Writing Part Time—For Fun and Money

by

Jack Clinton McLarn

First Printing - August, 1978

Library of Congress Number 78-50474
ISBN 0-913864-21-8

Published by
Enterprise Publishing Co.
501 Beneficial Building
Wilmington, Delaware 19801

TO MY WIFE

to Jackie and Bob, Scott, Mark and Chele Lane'
Daisy Bacon, Bob Bales, Ruth Beck, Rita Brenig,
Red Carey, Jean Chimsky, Virginia Cornwell,
Stanley Crane, Hellen Fain, A.L. Fierst,
Harriet Fortenberry, Dick Franklin,
Bob Hamilton, Margaret Hendrix,
Bernadette Hoyle, Freeman Hubbard, Mason King,
Beverly Kirby, Marjorie Layton, Henry Malmgreen,
Nicholas Monsarrat, Joe Moore, David Morgan,
Jim O'Connell, Hank Rames, Mary Rollins,
Robert Ruark, Ardis Sandel, Dan Senseney,
Cara Sherman, Susan Silverman,
Johanna Roman Smith, John Stover,
Macon Tolleson, Hill Trexler, Bill Wagner,
Ernie Weeks, Rhonda Wilson, Hilda Wright,
Bernie Young, and that host of others
whose patience, tolerance, understanding and
encouragement made it possible, this work is
respectfully, gratefully and affectionately
dedicated

-- *The Author*

Preface

This is not a serious book, nor is it a "How To Gain Fame And Fortune By Writing In Six Easy Lessons" treatise. Rather, it is the factual account of how one free-lancer, with an average education and little formal training in writing, managed to combine a career with such other vocations as railroad administrative officer, musician, composer, singer, instructor and lecturer in business and sales training, for nearly fifty years -- and have a whale of a lot of fun at the same time.

While it may appear to have been written primarily for the novice and sometime writer, the author hopes that this narration of his own experiences in the often confusing but always exhilirating "literary field" may make life a bit less complicated for anyone who may elect to venture down the same road.

Welcome -- friend!

J. C. McLarn

Contents

Foreword

Jack Clinton McLarn could have saved me from a lot of time and effort, and could have gotten me started earlier on my literary/journalistic career if he had produced WRITING PART TIME -- FOR FUN AND MONEY at least sixty years ago when I was a youngster obsessed with a desire to spread my wings as a free-lance writer.

What was urgently needed in those long-ago days were the viewpoints, the tips, and the short cuts to getting into print that this volume offers. Jack really should have written his book and sent me a copy of it at that early period in my life.

But Jack wasn't doing any writing at all at the time I needed such a book, except maybe with a piece of chalk on a school blackboard. If I had had a book like Jack's back when I was a fledgling writer, my road to success would have been a great deal smoother, and I dare say quicker.

As the editor of RAILROAD, I'm happy to say that Jack was the top fiction author on my magazine's Table of Contents page for many years. He is a skillful writer with a keen eye for the most discriminating detail. Let's say that he "knows whereof he speaks" in writing this informative book.

Jack McLarn is right. Writing can be (and is!) a lot of fun; in terms of the self-expression, achievement, satisfaction, and the notoriety it engenders. It is also profitable, if you go about it the right way. To do that, you need the kind of information this book can give you in terms of dealing with editors, submitting your material in suitable fashion, and maintaining professionalism.

So Jack's thesis makes sense; writing, whether it be part time or full time, can widen horizons and open the gates to fun and money.

I suggest to you, an aspiring author, that you use Jack McLarn's book as the scaffolding with which to build the edifice of your own writing career. And then, preferably even before that time, fill a notebook with materials of the type that you would like to write, garnered from your readings of good literature. A literary friend of mine, Elbert Hubbard, once said, "Keep the windows of your soul open toward the East, and some day the light will come."

WRITING PART TIME -- FOR FUN AND MONEY is a *vade mecum*, a manual or textbook, or literally, a "come with me." Add to it the wealth you have gained from your reading matter, jotted down beyond the reach of forgetfulness, and you *may* eventually awaken some fine sunny day to find yourself a successful author.

This book, in itself, will never get you anywhere if you simply read it and put it aside. Use it as a stepping stone -- an incentive. Or, to change the metaphor, regard yourself as a duck in a pond, calm on the surface, but paddling to beat hell underneath.

Freeman Hubbard, Editor
RAILROAD MAGAZINE

1 Writing as a Business

Interviewer: *Mr. McLarn, how did a man like you, with "Establishment" written all over him, ever get involved with something so far removed from "business" as writing? Just for fun?*
Me: *Young lady, I do very few things, including breathe, that I don't get some fun out of. Sure, I write for fun, and for money, too. But anybody who thinks writing isn't a "business" has a lot to learn.*

There is a hoary cliche to the effect that there are two kinds of writers – those who *write*, and those who want to *have written.*

To those who want-to-have-written, the writer is an artistic soul, and the ability to write is a heaven-sent gift. But to those who *write*, writing is definitely a business and one of the most exacting and demanding of all businesses, to be conducted within the bounds of solid business principles.

Some people are quite convinced that writers are really artists, whose facilities with words and phrases set them apart from everybody else, and that to dare imply that writing has "business aspects" is downright heresy. Writing is definitely a business, with all the frustrations, the problems, and the rewards of a business.

The writer is the owner and manager of a complicated, demanding business enterprise. They are the bosses and all of the employees. They are in business to produce something, and finally sell it in a highly competitive market. And they expect to make money out of it.

This premise applies whether the product is poetry or prose, fiction or fact, a little or a lot. It applies whether it is written for the "little books" that pay off in free copies, if at all, or for the mass circulation publications that send whopping checks. The writer is in business and must never forget it. Upon how well that business is conducted will determine whether the writers are wasting their time, efforts, talents or simply playing around with their blood pressure.

Suppose we do a little hard-nosed analyzing. Suppose we try to understand in what ways the writing business compares with a commercial business. Really, there isn't all that much difference.

First, in business of any kind, must come the basic idea. As the door-to-door salesman must get the "idea" of selling before starting to bug housewives with vacuum cleaners or Tupperware, so must the would-be writer somehow conceive and give birth to the "idea" of wanting to write, the conviction that the writer *can* write, and *must* write. Not to just *have written*, but to write.

So you already have the idea that you can and must write. Fine, but just as the salesperson must decide the kind of gadgets are to be sold, so must you decide what you are going to write; what you are going to produce; what "writing commodity" will be the foundation of your writing business.

So you're going to write articles. Fine again. But there are zillions of kinds of articles. Technical articles. Business articles. Inspirational articles. Religious articles. Personal experience articles. Historical articles. Have you ever tried to list how many different types of articles are published every month? I started such a list years ago. It still isn't complete. Never will be.

Maybe fiction is your bag. Excellent! The market for fiction -- *good* fiction, that is -- is terrific. But just what kind of fiction do you have in mind? Book-lengths, sixty thousand words or more? Short stories at five thousand words or less? Short-shorts at two thousand words a throw? Vignettes? Fillers?

And what kind of readers will you be writing for? Adults? Children? Kids?

Take your time about deciding. It's important. Eventually you'll settle on one general or specific category. Maybe more than one. The important thing right now is to establish a base of operations, a point from which to begin. Don't worry too much about becoming "typed" -- identified with a single area of literary effort. Many businesses are established for one purpose, and later diversify into entirely different fields. Countless writers do the same. I know because I'm one of them.

Inventory Your Assets

Once you have selected your business area, the next step is to "take inventory" of what you have to work with. The prospective manufacturer or retailer begins by taking stock; by inventorying the physical plant, equipment, facilities, furniture and fixtures, and personnel. The prospective writer must go and do likewise. So now sit down and ask yourself some pointed questions, such as:

> "Do I have the education and the ability to write a cohesive, literate sentence, paragraph, series of related paragraphs?"
>
> "Do I have at least a basic knowledge of the rules of grammar -- high school or better?"

"Do I write and speak correctly by instinct? Or do I have to think too much about what I am writing or saying -- so much that I sometimes lose the thread of what I'm trying to say or write?"

"Do the words I write describe the pictures in my mind? Will they convey those same pictures to the mind of my readers? Do they convey impressions, stir emotions?"

"Do I have ready access to an up-to-date encyclopedia, a good dictionary, a Bartlett's Quotations, a thesaurus, and a Bible? Do I know how to use them?"

"Do I have a good typewriter -- and can I type with reasonable speed and accuracy?"

"Do I have the patience and the stamina to spend long, lonely, frustrating hours staring at a blank piece of paper and a sneering typewriter keyboard, trying to find a way out of the mess into which I have somehow written my characters, and myself?"

If it scares you, welcome to the club. I still get goosebumps when I do a self-analysis job on myself. It can be a downright traumatic experience. And what I've just laid on you is only the beginning. It gets worse. Much worse.

Make a Market Survey

Before committing oneself too deeply in whatever business one elects to enter, the businessperson determines the market potential for the product or service. They make what they refer to as a "market survey." They gather information as to the areas into which they are about to direct their efforts.

The writers must also decide where their own best possibilities for success may lie. They have a lot of market research data available to them. There are several writing magazines, such as AUTHOR AND JOURNALIST, THE PENWOMAN, THE WRITER, WRITER'S DIGEST, which publish regularly updated columns as to the needs of various publishers. WRITER'S MARKET, published by WRITER'S DIGEST is available at most libraries and contains indexed and classified analyses of practically every magazine and book publisher in this country and others. It gives types of material wanted, wordage, payment, where to send manuscripts, how to prepare manuscripts, and a lot of related information designed to make the life of the writer, novice or old pro, a lot more bearable.

But even with all this help, writers have a lot of study and decision making ahead of them. As no business person would think of taking in too much territory, no writer should try to turn out material for more than a few of the hundreds of possible publishers. No business person would specialize the product to such an extent as to unduly limit the marketing potential. Neither should beginning or long-time professionals select such a narrow field that the possible outlets for the material are too few, too low-paying, or too hard to satisfy. They should allow themselves room to maneuver; in a field where something that may not suit one editor may well be just right for an editor on the next floor in the same building. The beginning writer should start in a field where there are several publishers. It is pretty disheartening to write a good piece for a limited, highly specialized market, get a "sorry, but..." reject, and find that there isn't any place to try the same material again. It has happened to me. But not any more. I make certain that there is a back-up market for just about everything I write.

It is at this point in the development of the budding writing business that policy-making becomes a factor; where the success or failure of the enterprise may well be determined. "Marketing Research" is often the basis for this policy making.

The current WRITER'S MARKET lists some twenty-two titles in the "Confessions" category, but there are really many more on the newsstands. They use several hundred stories just about every month. This would seem to provide a pretty broad marketing area for the beginning writer. All Confessions being pretty much alike, the writer may reason, any fairly well done tale in the "Sin, Suffer, Repent" tradition should sell to one of these publications. So the writer reads a few back issues, dashes off six thousand words or so of "God-How-I-Suffer!" prose -- including a few eyebrow-raising sex episodes -- and fires the script off to the magazine that WRITER'S MARKET says offers the most cents per word. Then, when the script comes back with embarrassing promptness and a form-letter rejection, the writer ships it out again and again, completely unable to understand the stupidity of the PhD's who moonlight as readers in the "Confessex" field in not recognizing exceptional material -- especially when friends keep saying how good the stories are.

In industry this would be called "Inadequate Market Analysis." The decision to specialize in the Confessions may have been perfectly sound. The Confessions provide one of the best training grounds in the writing profession. But in this instance, where the writer's Market Research Department goofed was in not thoroughly researching the market -- in not determining the subtle differences in the feel of the various Confession books. Only a dispassionately serious study of individual styles and content of the various magazines, including sending for their free "Writers' Guide Lines," can reveal to the writer what touches and incidents are acceptable in one, yet will draw a by-return-mail rejection from another. Nobody, not even WRITER'S DIGEST or WRITER'S MARKET, can help you much there. Your own Director of Marketing Research will have to get on the ball. And who might that be? You.

Production Control and Cost Control

"Production Control" and "Cost Control" are industrial engineering terms, related to any modern business enterprise. And if you're wondering whether the publishers haven't gotten pages from a manual on Industrial Engineering or Business Administration mixed up with this "writing book," relax. They haven't.

Production Control consists of the supervision of the manufacture of the product in any business, from the time the components go into the assembly line, throughout the various processes of manufacture, down to when the finished product goes out the door.

"Cost Control" is a term applied to a means of preventing the Production Department from spending so much time and material on manufacturing an item that the selling price of the item is less than the cost, or so close to it as to make profit unlikely, or so small as to not be worth the effort.

In industry this isn't hard to calculate. Material cost + labor cost + overhead = total cost. The selling price must be set high enough to show a reasonable profit over and above that total cost figure. All very simple.

But the cost factor in your writing business isn't based upon such a simple formula. True, the basics, the paper, typewriter ribbons, repairs, etc., are cost elements. Typing time, research time, even "thinking time" can be measured down to the minute, and priced accordingly. But there are intangibles that cannot be costed out. There is no way to put a price upon knowledge, know-how and experience -- those assets that may have taken you years to acquire. Absolutely no way.

I once took on an assignment at a flat fee -- nice money, too. But after I delivered the script, and figured out what it had cost me to produce it in time, material, letters of inquiry, digging through reference books, writing and re-writing, I found that the same time and effort running a bulldozer would have paid me far more than the "fee" for which I had all but battered my brains out. And running one of those behemoths would have been more fun, too!

It's easy to see what went wrong. My Cost Control Department just didn't do its job. It permitted me to take on a project without first costing it out, without making at least a horseback estimate of what the job would require. It was humiliating, too, to think that I had done all that hard work for such a small return. Unless a writer wants to write just for the sheer satisfaction of "having written something," a time-and-energy-consuming-peanuts-paying assignment is little better than no assignment at all. It would be more profitable to go out and wash the windows, or edge the lawn. I have this posted on the wall over my typewriter -- *When I take on an assignment, I will know what it is going to cost me to do it, and what I will get out of it before I commit myself.* Let it be so with you.

Quality Control

"Quality Control," a term relatively new in industry, refers to insuring the worthiness of the product; to detecting and correcting faulty materials and workmanship. In any business, and especially in the writing business, Quality Control is nothing more than seeing that a good job is done in every instance. Quality Control in writing may include such things as using a fresh typewriter ribbon, producing a sharp, black impression rather than a faded grey one; using a good grade of hard-finish paper (which some editors don't like), from which an eraser will remove a letter, a word, or a whole sentence, without leaving a smudge. It also includes observing standard manuscript format as to margins, page numbers, word-count; laying a completed manuscript aside to cool for a day or so, then going over it, not as an adoring parent cooing over a new-born child, but with the coldly critical eye of an editor with a hangover and a naturally mean disposition. Seeing that nouns and verbs agree; that double and triple adverbs aren't overworked. That cliches are "avoided like the plague." That you haven't changed the name of the character in the middle of the yarn. That no two names begin with the same letter, or sound too much alike. That a nice character doesn't suddenly turn into a louse for no apparent reason.

Quality Control in writing is the same as in any business -- insurance against shoddy production.

2 Writing as a Business (Continued)

Selling and Marketing

"Selling" and "Marketing," terms also widely used in business, are often considered to mean the same thing. They do not.

Selling is often considered in the dictionary sense, as the "act of transferring property to another for money," the sale being regarded as strictly a one-time operation, not likely to be repeated. Marketing, however, implies a more meaningful relationship between the seller and the buyer -- even going so far as to include changing the product to meet the needs of the customer, the buyer.

An editor recently returned one of my scripts with a somewhat snippy note to the effect that it "violated one of her pet taboos." The point was really a nit-picker, and had I been only interested in making a sale, I would have simply sent it out to a back-up market, with no changes, where it would probably have sold. Instead, I re-wrote the offending passages, changed the ending a bit -- "reworked the product to meet the objections of the customer" -- and sent it back to the lady, thanking her for her "astute criticism," and asking her to take another look at the revisions I had made at her suggestion.

Her by-return-mail acceptance note included, "Well! Am I surprised! A writer not too thin-skinned to take criticism and not too lazy to re-write! Send me more, okay?"

That's a fair example of the business principle of Marketing as applied to the business of writing. Marketing is the giving of assurance to the customer -- in this instance, a tough lady editor -- that the manufacturer (me) cared more about establishing a reputation than making one measly sale.

There are other subtle ways to establish a good marketing relationship with your customers -- the editors. For instance, making the packaging of your product more attractive. Some of the writing manuals say it's okay to send manuscripts folded, and to use small envelopes for return. Could be. But using 9½ x 12½ inch envelopes, mailing all manuscripts flat, with 9 x 12 inch pre-addressed and *adequately* stamped envelopes inside for return, is certainly more businesslike -- and more impressive, too. Another thing -- use fresh envelopes. "Re-cycling" envelopes may be ecologically sound, but they don't do much for your image in the editorial shops.

About that little matter of return postage. I once omitted sending return postage with a manuscript. I got it back -- postage collect -- (legal then) -- with a blistering note from the editor, calling me "the worst kind of amateur!" It took me six months to get him to even look at one of my scripts again. Don't make *that* mistake. It'll cost you.

Should return postage be stuck onto the return envelope? Definitely. I used to paper-clip stamps to the return envelope. But I started getting manuscripts back "postage due," which didn't help my status with my mail man. Now I stick the stamps to the return envelope. If the script sells, I certainly don't begrudge the publisher's mail room person a few free stamps.

Another gimmick to make your submissions more professional is the use of "pressure sensitive" labels for addressing manuscript envelopes. They come in a dozen sizes, all completely legal. For return addresses on envelopes I use those little thousand-for-a-buck gummed printed labels. They're a lot more convenient than crowding a long envelope into a short-carriage typewriter and trying to type a return address on it.

These little touches will tell your editors that you are a no-fooling-around professional, and will boost your image as a writer who knows his business, and who respects the editors, his customers, as fellow professionals.

I don't do anything that I even think can give an editor or any of his cohorts the slightest reason for regarding me unkindly. More than one of them has told me that any extra handling they have to give a script prejudices them just that much against the writer. One said, "We try to be businesslike in this shop. We expect you characters to be businesslike, too!"

Production Scheduling and Control

To make money in a writing business, even in the nickel-a-word-or-better bracket, the writer must maintain a fairly consistent production schedule. That means keeping scripts coming and going right sharply. He needs a quick, easy method of keeping up with his wandering brain-children – and to avoid sending a rejected script back to the same editor who rejected it. I've done this. Darned if one editor didn't buy the same yarn she had nixed only weeks before. Unfortunately, somebody reminded her. She's still mad at me.

When I complete a manuscript, I make a 3 x 5 index card for it, noting the title, the kind of piece, the number of words, where I send it, and the date. If it comes back, I note the date rejected, and when and where it is remailed, repeating the process until the script sells, or until I decide it is hopeless.

If the script sells, I note on the card who bought it, date and price, and drop it into the "Sold-But-Not-Paid-For" slot in my dime-store tin box. When I get paid, I note the date and amount on the card, and transfer it into the "Sold-And-Paid-For" section of the box. If I give up on it as unsalable, I put the card into the "Inventory" slot in the box. However, having the instincts of a disorderly pack-rat, I never throw a script away, sold or unsold. Browsing through long-ago sold or retired scripts often triggers brand-new story ideas. Too, I occasionally get inquiries from new editors, asking if I have any "rejects" they can consider. I always do have them. Some they buy, too.

Accounting, Bookkeeping -- and Taxes

At a recent seminar I was asked how I coped with my tax problems. It flattered me no end to think that somebody believed I had a tax problem, but it was a good question. Any self-employed individual can throw away money if there isn't a meticulous record of income and expenses involved in writing activities. Thanks to the Internal Revenue Service, there are guide-lines to use in keeping such records.

I know I needn't remind you that there is such a thing as a tax on your Self-Employment income, over and above your regular personal income tax. This tax builds up your Social Security, and while it may seem of little consequence to younger people, to Senior Citizens such as this one it may mean the difference between dignity and discomfort.

I strongly urge that you acquire a standard tax book. I use one such as COMMERCE CLEARING HOUSE, PRENTICE-HALL, LASSER, PORTER, in addition to the publications of the IRS. They will tell you about such things as charging off the room in your home you use for your writing, depreciation on your equipment, travel expense, improving your writing skills by attending seminars, taking courses, buying books -- all deductions from your writing income. But only if you can show that you are writing with the expectation of making a profit, and not merely as a hobby. The only way to prove this is by keeping records. A small ledger will do. Put down postage, stationery, supplies, etc.; keep receipts, noting on them what they cover. If your tax return is ever audited, the IRS people can be downright unneighborly unless you have the records to back up your claim.

Those who share my Senior Citizen status will readily understand why I make such a thing of taking all the deductions to which we are entitled. Here's why.

Starting in a recent year, you can earn up to $4,000 (up from $3,000 previously) without losing some benefits. Earn more than that, you lose a dollar of benefits for every two you earn in excess of the annual limits, even if you work only a month. This earnings limitation will rise each year until it reaches $6,000. After that, no earnings limit will apply to people age 70 or older.

The importance of this is obvious. If you get lucky, and make a lot of sales, the smart thing to do is to take all the deducts you can from your writing income, so when you reach the bottom line it reflects only your actual profit. Your friendly local Social Security or Railroad Retirement Board Administrator will explain this to you better than I can.

Another bright spot is that eventually Senior Citizens over 70, as compared with the current age 72, can earn all their arthritis will permit without losing any of their hard-earned income.

It makes sense to keep accurate records of how many hours you work, what you earn, and what it costs you to earn it. It makes no sense whatever to find that you are working for literally nothing.

Public Relations For The Writer

Industry spends a lot of money and effort on Public Relations; on the image of the concern as a good neighbor. The writer should also be an active participant in the community.

Writing is one of the few businesses in which the practitioners not only tolerate newcomers, but actively encourage them. Early in my writing career I wrote a lot of pretty brash letters to some big-name writers. Not one brush-off did I get. Instead, I received many replies, some of them veritable essays on writing -- as a craft, an art, even as a business. I did receive some letters describing writing as a "racket," and an "abomination," along with one scrawled, unsigned note calling the profession a "damned disease, voluntarily contracted by blasted idiots like you!"

Writers will do well to share their specialized knowledge, talents, and experience with those who may one day be privileged to do the same, by speaking at writing conferences and clubs, helping in amateur writing contests, writing and editing neighborhood garden club news-letters, church and community papers. But mostly by just being interested, available and helpful among those who find writing so fascinating -- just as you must have, when you first felt the writing urge.

But being helpful can have drawbacks. It can bring letters, calls, visits from people who, ". . . have a wonderful idea for a story! I'll tell it to you, all you have to do is write it, and I'll give you some of the money I get for it!" It can also bring you what a charming little old lady once sent me, along with a box of cookies -- a handwritten script which could have come straight out of Sunnybrook Farm, along with a note asking me to, "Put some of your love scenes in this, sell it under your name, and send me the money."

Be helpful, yes. But not that helpful!

Evaluation -- At The Executive Level

It is the responsibility of the head of any business to periodically evaluate the effectiveness of that business; to determine whether it is operating at a profit or a loss; and to decide upon what changes may be necessary, as well as to forecast the prospects of the enterprise.

It is not enough for you, the head of your writing business, to merely total up your sales. Honest evaluation demands much more of you.

I'm often asked what I consider to be a "regular contributor" to magazines. That, in itself, is a form of evaluation. I usually say something like, 'Regular Contributors' are writers who sell more scripts than they get back."

Surprised that an "old pro" would admit to getting rejects? Don't be. We all do. I evaluate my sales record this way: "Send out ten, get four back, fair. Three back, good! Two back -- Genius!" Sell ten out of ten? Not me.

When I was younger, I took vindictive pleasure in submitting and re-submitting the same script until somebody finally bought it, maybe for half a cent a word. This is okay, if you're just playing at writing. But it's poor business not to consider the financial angle, even if you're having a ball. Whatever personal satisfaction you may get out of proving a lot of editors wrong and one right is more than offset by the time, material and postage you waste, which could be better used to prepare and submit new, fresh material -- or the time used to figure out what was wrong with the piece in the first place that made so many editors hold their collective noses.

My "submission evaluation index" is that a script deserves five trials before being revised, or retired. As I said before, I never scrap a manuscript. It may contain an idea, a scene, a phrase that I can use somewhere. So, to borrow a computer term, I feed the script into my 'memory bank,' to be retrieved on one of those ghastly days when the typewriter and I stare at one another for hours, with neither of us saying a word.

Your evaluation method should be one that is meaningful to you. Perhaps I can offer some suggestions as to how to develop an evaluation formula and procedure. Ask yourself these questions:

"How many scripts have I sent out during the past six

months, compared with the six months before?"

"How many sold in each period?"

"How many sold first time out? Second? Third?"

"How many sold for five cents a word, or better? Four cents? Three cents? Less than three cents?"

"To what markets do I sell most consistently?"

"How many printed rejections did I get, and how many personal notes?"

"How many editors use my first name in their letters?"

"How many editors suggested revisions?"

"How many of these revisions sold?"

"Do I read my own published words without wondering why I wrote such a stupid thing?"

Finally, and probably the most important of all:

"Am I really having fun doing this?"

Take this test every few months; write the answers down, put them away, look at them once in a while. Do you change from test to test? You just might learn something about your writing from this procedure. You'll certainly learn something about yourself.

The Role of the Literary Agent

Earlier I said that the writer is "the owner and manager of a complicated, demanding business enterprise . . . the boss and all of the employees." Correction: They may have one "employee" -- rather, associate -- beside themselves.

Before I was to speak at a writing seminar not a long time ago, I found an unsigned note in my hotel mail box. "Talk about Agents," it read.

There is as much dynamite in those three words as there might be in an abandoned car on the streets of Belfast. Probably no other topic generates as much controversy when writers get together. To adequately cover all the angles of this explosive subject would take more time and space than I want to use. But I will say this -- my experience with Literary Agents has been excellent.

Literary Agents are highly skilled professionals. Many are former top-drawer writers, and bring into the field of author representation an impeccable knowledge of writing and related problems. Others have been editors, lawyers, college professors. They have one thing in common. They know writers and writing as few of us can ever hope to know them. They offer to the writer the benefits of years of experience -- in writing, publishing, selling, editing -- in every phase of the writing craft.

Agents fall into two general categories; those whose services are not readily available to the unproven writer, and those who are willing to work with novice writers.

Agents in the first group usually get their new clients through referrals by their regular clients, rarely by direct solicitation. They want to represent only writers of demonstrated capability, and potential profit to the Agent. They usually expect the prospective client to have a track record of sales to national publications, or a non-"vanity house" published book, and, in the judgement of the Agent, the ability to produce consistently salable material.

This makes sense. The Agent spends a lot of time reading and evaluating material; publishers look to Agents to screen scripts for them, practically doing the work of a house reader. Agents know that when they submit a script to a publisher, they are putting their own literary reputation behind it.

The others, the so-called "Advertising Agents," are, in my opinion, subjected to a lot of unjustified static. They offer tyros the same general service as that provided by the non-advertisers. In the past, most Advertising Agents charged a reading fee for reviewing and evaluating manuscripts. This fee pays for an analysis of the writers' material, often pages long, including the Agent's criticism from a professional standpoint, an opinion as to the salability of the scripts, suggestions as to revision, and sometimes blunt statements of the Agent's estimate of the writer's potential. More recently, some Agents advertise "no reading fee," but I have seen contracts that include what are called "representation fees" for new writers, to be refunded as and when the writer's material begins to sell. This, in effect, is a reading fee in a new guise.

Agents who charged reading fees usually dropped the fees after making a couple of sales for the client. Some Agents in both fields require long-term contracts, sometimes obligating the writer to submit all work through the Agency. I do not fault them for that. Agents spend their time, use their contacts and knowledge to develop the writer, and it is only fair that they should benefit from their efforts when the writer does well. But, as with any long-term contract in any business, the writer should not sign a contract with an Agent or anyone else without understanding just what it means -- and just what it will take to terminate the relationship. I still remember the exasperated lady who told me, and everybody else within earshot, "I could get rid of my husband easier than I could get out of my contract with that Agent!"

In my early writing days I had a full-time job, so I didn't

have time to both write and sell. So I turned to one of the Advertising Agents. He was one of the better ones. He sold my scripts when they were salable, ripped them and me to bits when they weren't. He kept me informed on markets, got me increases in word-rates, took me to see editors in buildings where I couldn't have gotten past the elevator starter on my own; invited me to his posh home, served me ten-year-old brandy, broiled me a steak, made me feel as though I were the only client he had. I still send him clients, and we still exchange reminiscent letters about the "old days."

There are Agents who offer to revise, even re-write scripts, for whopping fees, with no guarantee of a sale. Others have "writing schools" on the side. Nothing wrong with either, so long as the writers they work with understand the relationship, and know what they may expect from it.

There are also the tales about writers being taken by the "sharpies" who seem to attach themselves to every profession. I've even looked into some of the more lurid incidents. In just about every such case, the victim (self-styled) was miffed because the Agent he was villifying was bluntly honest enough to tell the would-be Hemingways to quit wasting their money and everybody's time trying to be what they weren't, and go try something more suited to their talents and abilities.

My long-time Agency friend told me this, "Writers need an Agent only to do what they can't or won't do for themselves."

He was so right. My own career proves it. What writing I do now is in specialized fields, in which I am something of an authority. I usually have specific assignments, with much editorial direction, so I have little need for agency representation -- in that particular area.

However, as embarrassing as it is to admit it, several years ago I became involved with a publisher in a field totally foreign to anything within my experience. I contracted to prepare a recording script, on a royalty basis. I prepared the script, it was produced superbly, and I sat back to await my royalties. What happened? Another firm took over the "assets but not the liabilities" of the contracting firm. The new firm is selling the tapes for which I prepared the scripts, even using them in advertising, and I have never been paid a cent. And probably never will be.

I have mentally kicked myself around several blocks for getting into such a ridiculous situation. Had I exhibited the good sense to send the whole matter to my Agency friend, he would have handled the whole matter, I would have been paid. Instead, here I am, with egg on my face, months of work wasted, bales of information used, all because I didn't do what my common sense should have told me to do. If I ever do such a foolish thing again, I hope somebody sends for the men in the white coats.

Whether to work through an Agent is one of the many executive decisions to be made by the writer. WRITER'S MARKET lists scads of Agents, and the services they offer. The writing magazines' advertisements show in detail what the writer may expect from the Agents who advertise in them.

I have been asked many times how a writer should go about getting an Agent. The only answer I ever give goes something like this:

> "First, convince yourself that you really want an Agent. Then, do one of two things.
>
> > "Address inquiries to several of the 'Advertising Agents'; tell them your background, what you want to do in writing, send them what you consider your best work, and request an opinion as to your prospects as a writer. Compare the replies, and you will know pretty well which of the Agents will be best for you.
> >
> > "Try to sell a few scripts on your own. The contact with editors, even if only by rejection slips, will give

you good experience, as well as the 'feel' of writing. Then, if you do make a few sales, approach a couple of the Non-Advertising Agents, cite your sales record, and ask for consideration.

"But remember this. The relationship between Agent and writer is a very personal one. Agents will give you their best efforts, and they will expect yours. If you do make any kind of an Agency connection, be prepared to listen to what the Agent says. Don't argue. Do what they say to do. Your interests are theirs. Let them do their job their way, for their ten percent. Don't expect miracles. Do expect criticism, discipline, even discouragement. There is no easy road to writing success. No way!"

I had some misgivings about using the "Industrial Engineering" and "Business Principle" approach in making my points in the chapters just concluded. But I am firmly convinced that business methods and business principles have definite places in even so ethereal an area as that of writing. My own writing career would have never gotten off the ground without them. And if what I say sounds coldly cynical; if it seems to reduce the "art of writing" to a "crass, crude, 'business proposition'" (as an irate person once told me after one of my seminar talks) then I'm sorry. But despite the profit motive and the commercialism I may seem to stress, there are profits in writing that can never show up in a profit and loss statement, a balance sheet, or an income tax return. Not the least of those profits is the inner glow of satisfaction that even a small sale brings, along with the fun of trying.

3 Confessions of a Confession Writer

Interviewer: *Mr. McLarn, how did a man who looks like a school teacher, talks like a politician, turns red at four-letter words, get into writing (bleep!) like Confessions?*

Me: *How? Or why? Because they're good discipline for a writer; they're fun to write; and they pay up to a nickel a word.*

When that personable young woman and her tape recorder turned up at my home to talk to me about writing, I had no idea of what I was letting myself in for. Since that interview was published, I've been discussed at length by the members of the Bible Class I teach, the target of odd looks from my wife's bridge-playing friends, stifled giggles from the neighborhood teen-agers, and snide comments from just about everybody else.

As I told the reporter, Confessions are not the only things I write. But since that interview, even if I had written the Book of Genesis, all anybody seems to remember about me is that I'm that "... old geezer down the block who writes those sexy tales for those awful Confession Magazines." Nobody seems to know anything about my educational writing, my tales for kids, management and sales training courses, church treatises, my work with children and adults with speech difficulties. Nobody. I'm typed, forever and amen.

No, I didn't start out writing for the Confessions. Some of my early writing, however, was for what were then called "Romance Publications." Few people today remember the Street & Smith LOVE STORY MAGAZINE of the 1930's, a pulp-paper magazine edited by a charming lady named, appropriately enough, "Daisy." Miss Daisy Bacon.

Stories for Miss Daisy had to be sugar-and-spice sweet, and super-clean. About the most exciting scene she would tolerate might include a tenderly pressed hand, or possibly a single brief, chastely antiseptic kiss right at the end of a story, preferably just before or after the wedding of the main characters. Paragraphs with the slightest purple tinge uspet her terribly, and she would blue-pencil even a mild "darn!" if uttered by a female character. It was Miss Daisy who bought and published my first fiction. Thirty-five hundred words, thirty-five dollars. An Author Was Born!

Confession Books as we know them today came into being before 1920. They were daringly experimental, and by today's standards, very mild. After a few sales to the soft-soap Romance Publications, I decided to try the new medium, despite dire warnings about their "lack of respectability." The Confessions of that day were a bit easier to write for than were the Romance books -- and, to my pop-eyed amazement, my first Confession check equalled four of the "sweetness-and-light" pay-offs.

The Confession editors of those days were pretty formula conscious. Their stories had to be from the female viewpoint, with a female first-person narrator, who always got into a jam -- because of misplaced trust, mistaken judgement, misguided love, or just plain stupidity. The usual "mistake" was one involving unmarried pregnancy, or some equally horrifying circumstance common to that era, such as a brutal uncle, cruel step-mother, etc. The narrator had to suffer inward agony for five thousand words or so, and then somehow "solve her problem." Stories and characterizations had to be tenth-grade simple, and the outcome always tearfully happy, happy, happy.

After a few months of this sort of thing, I tried the "he-man" field. It wasn't so easy as the Confessions, but it paid even better, and gave me a by-line, boosting my adolescent ego no end. Now I could tell people I was a selling writer, and prove it.

My railroad background was an inexhaustible source of material. For several years I had a lot of fun, and made good money writing two-fisted action stories for ARGOSY, ADVENTURE, RAILROAD MAGAZINE, and other pulps and slicks, and thought I had it made – even considering quitting my railroad job and going full-time into writing.

I was lucky. My more practical-minded wife knocked that nonsense out of my inflated head with a few well-chosen words. For, in the early 1950's, the books for which I ground out stacks of hard-boiled, man-against-nature, man-against-man, man-against-himself fiction either folded or changed dramatically. High adventure, male-oriented stuff -- even my old stand-by, railroad fiction – dried up completely, replaced by the "true-to-life" era. Situations, themes, incidents that had once been strictly taboo became commonplace. The pages of printed stories dwindled; in their stead came pages of sexy, anatomically explicit photographs. We writers of adventure-action material had a choice. Convert to the "new mode," or quit.

I quit. And for several years remained quit. But once the writing bug gets into a writer's system, it never leaves, even though it might remain dormant for years. So I decided to try once more. The only "big" market left seemed to be the modern-day version of the Confessions. So I bought a dozen back issues at random, holed up in a beach cottage belonging to a sympathetic friend, and did some hard-nosed research.

I got a shock. The Confessions had changed. And *how* they changed!

There remained on the mast-heads not one single editor I had known from the old days. The new editors wouldn't even look at the low-key, piddlingly unsensational problem tales of the type I had waded through years before. The writing had changed, too. The genteel, romantic love scenes were out. The "in" thing was sex. Sex that went far beyond the rigid limits imposed thirty years before. Where once the writer could imply much by simply inserting a few dots . . . . . at the strategic points in the tale . . . . . , the new editors demanded to know everything, in almost clinical detail. "Problems" were acceptable, but they had become medical, psychological, psychiatric, treating almost casually such things as sexual maladjustment, nymphomania, homosexuality, lesbianism, fetishism -- the gamut of human foibles, normal and abnormal. My seaside research told me with grisly frankness that the "New Confessions" were really confessions -- about life with no holds barred, no punches pulled. Life, with the bark on and the clothing scattered all over the bedroom floor -- or the den, or the kitchen!

During the interview that got me started to writing this book, the reporter-inquisitor asked me if I knew who the first Confession Writer was. That was probably the only easy question she asked me all afternoon.

The first Confession Writer was probably the one who wrote:

> *"But that I am forbid*
> *To tell the secrets of my prison-house,*
> *I could a tale unfold, whose lightest word*
> *Would harrow up thy soul, freeze thy young blood;*
> *Make thy two eyes, like stars,*
> *Start from their spheres;*
> *Thy knotted and combine locks to part*
> *And each particular hair to stand on end*
> *Like quills upon the fretful porcupine . . .* "

A Confession Story written to this ancient formula will sell to just about any of the Confession Books on the stands today. Bill Shakespeare was probably the patron saint of the Confession industry.

Today's Confession editors are among the best in the business. They know exactly what they want, what their readers want, and aren't a bit hesitant in demanding it of their writers. They tell us so, as evidenced from a few of the letters I still have.

> *"Ours is a behavior magazine that I feel serves a definite social need. Our readers depend upon these stories to aid them in solving their own problems. They demand a moral . . . one by which they can guide their own lives. They seek to 'identify', and thereby learn from the experience of others in their same social and economic sphere . . . "*

> *"The young women who read our magazine have constantly demonstrated that they look to the magazine as a 'textbook of life', far removed from the sales stimulating covers, titles and blurbs. These people have real problems that cannot be merely swept under the rug. Daily they must face problems of courtship and marriage, infidelity, financial disaster, fatherless children, adultry, alcoholism, cruelty, 'teen-age confusion, in a rapidly changing world . . . They run the full spectrum of human experience . . ."*

> *"Our readers demand down-to-earth stories embracing old-fashioned morality -- stories of good and evil, of faith in God, and regardless of erring, a sound faith in basic goodness. They demand that all sin and evil in these stories be punished, but that a ray of hope for the future be left in the end . . . "*

> *". . . These facts are borne out in the thousands of grateful letters we receive thanking us for the realistic and moralistic way our stories are handled . . ."*

From an editor, about the first story she took from me:

"Let me congratulate you on a darned good story! This is really well done, and meets the requirements of our book. Many thanks -- more of your work, please! This is the first story of yours I've seen, and I'm indeed pleased at your ability to tell a story, and make it ring true. It is unusual for a man to write from the woman's viewpoint and still come across. Mostly it can be detected, but this one fooled us all! If you do have this type of story from a man's viewpoint, we can use those, too!"

But in the next mail this came:

"Sorry -- plot seemed too obviously contrived -- characters not as believable as they might have been -- try us again, huh?"

That nasty word, "contrived" will constantly rise to confound you, all through your writing career. The dictionary meaning is, "To plan ingeniously; devise. To plot; scheme. To manage, as by some device or scheme . . ." I once asked an editor just what she meant when she said one of my plots was "too contrived."

"McLarn," she wrote, "Whenever one of your characters solves her problems too easily, or gets out of a jam too conveniently, I get the feeling that you thought up the answer first, and then asked the question. No way, mister. You can write your detective stories backward, but not for me."

"Contrived." "Not believable" -- the continuing complaints of the Confession editors. They tell you a lot about the confessing business.

From another editor, now retired, who became one of my best friends:

"Can you take a little deflating? Somehow or other, stories always bog down when they get into a courtroom,

unless they are (1) written by an expert on courtroom procedure, and (2) amenable to full-length treatment that will milk the subject for all the potential drama and suspense. Neither of these conditions is met here -- or, at any rate, if you really are a courtroom expert, it doesn't come through. And the narrator loses stature as the tale progresses, for clinging to her love for the guy long after it has become apparent that he's a jerk, just as her roomie says . . .Sorry -- no sale . . ."

I didn't tell my critical editor-friend that I once moonlighted as a court stenographer, and that the scene he found so "unconvincing" came word-for-word from my shorthand notes of a particularly messy rape case. I learned long ago not to argue with an editor. Their memories are too long. Besides, it is a basic premise of all business relations that the "customer is always right." So is the editor.

The foregoing excerpts were taken at random from among the dozens of letters from the Confession editors that have come my way. I wish I had kept them all. I could probably use them to write a whole volume on "How to Write Confessions in Six Easy Lessons," and make myself a bundle. But even cherished possessions disappear in the constant moves of a railroad man, so not many of them survived. But it was those editors, the ladies and gentlemen of the Confessions, who made me into a Confess Writer, by their patience, their understanding, and their always good-humored advice and counsel.

Writing today's Confession Story requires three basics. A certain amount of writing skill; a certain psychological insight into what makes people tick; and a certain ability to write in the style that the editors feel will hold the attention of their particular class of readers.

A Confession Story is nothing more than the "problem" story of long ago -- with a beginning, a middle, and an end, not necessarily in that order -- but considerably hopped up. Some modern writers -- good ones, too -- seem to have forgotten these ABC's of writing. But the Confession editors haven't, and they make sure that their writers do no forget them, either. They look for three broad concepts of story telling.

First, a *definite, readily discernible plot*, but not a complicated one. There should be no counter-plot. The basic plot must be strong enough to make the reader want to know, and care about, everything that happens to the characters. One editor wrote me, "*Things kept happening to these kids -- that's what sold me the story . . .*" Another editor told me that her linotype operator became so interested in the narrator of one of my emotion-packed yarns that he quit setting it up, and read the manuscript to the end, to find out how the girl narrator got out of the mess she was in. And one lady editor wrote me that I, "*almost had her crying!*"

The key-words in the foregoing paragraph are these: "Happening." "Interest." "Emotion." These three factors are necessary in any Confession Story. Too, the "story line" should be one carrying appeal for a widely varied audience. The "every-day housewife" the country-western singers wail about, who wants nothing more than to get off her aching feet for a little while and lose herself in the troubles of somebody worse off than she is. The little hash-house waitresses ready to do anything to get away from the pawing hands and leering propositions. The mini-skirted office girl with a yen for her married boss. The teen-ager who doesn't want to go "all the way," yet fears losing her boy friend because he demands that she "prove her love." In every instance the plot must be one the reader can understand without too many mental gymnastics, and the narrator must be someone with whom the reader can readily identify. When a reader thinks, "*Why, that could have been me!*", the writer has done his job.

Second on the editorial want-list is characterization. Stock, colorless, predictable characters come a dime a dozen. Confession readers want the narrator and the supporting cast in the story to seem to be real people, capable of doing things right, but also capable of human blunders. I've had scripts come back to me with such comments as:

> *"This gal never comes alive. What is she? A marble statue?"*
>
> *"I just don't believe this girl ever existed, except in McLarn's fevered imagination. She's just plain silly!"*

"Come alive." "Believe." Key words in the Confession lexicon. Memorize them. Use them.

Okay -- so how do you make the characters in a Confession believable? It isn't easy, but, with a little study, it can be done. Try this gimmick. Write a one-page description of the character, just as she comes to your mind, just as you would be describing her to a friend. Include her physical attributes -- well-stacked or not, for example -- the color of her hair and eyes, her home background, her education, what she likes and doesn't like, whatever turns her on or leaves her cold -- whatever you can think of that will make her more *real* to you. Do this, and she will become *real* in your mind -- and that reality will grow as she tells her story. Or you can model her after someone you know -- her personality, the way she talks, walks, etc. But don't be too accurate. I once fashioned a narrator after a cute little next-door neighbor, referring to her as a "natural red-head." When the story came out, I had the devil's own time explaining to her husband -- and to my wife -- how I knew she was a "natural red-head!"

Editors insist upon *characters from the main-stream of life.* Sales-girls. Car-hops. High school kids. Store and office clerks. Stay-at-home-and-hate-it housewives. If you use high fashion models, finishing-school grads, country club types. you're asking for rejects. Have a look at some of mine. *"Too upper-middle-class for us." "This broad moves in too fancy circles for my readers."* And this classic, *"How the hell can my readers identify with a gal wearing a mink coat and going to the country club in a Mercedes to play high-stake bridge? I publish 'Confessions', not Cosmopolitan!"*

I changed the life-styles of the people in these rejected stories and sold them on the next try, proving something -- I'm not too sure just what. But my judgement isn't always so good, either. One so-so tale had been rejected by all my usual markets. On impulse, I sent it, without a cover letter, to the top book in the Confession field. It drew a check and a laudatory letter from an editor to whom I'd never before sold a line. When I analyzed the piece to see why what I thought was a complete dud made such a hit with a prestigious publication, it dawned upon me that I had experimented with giving my narrator some unusual quirks of characterization I'd never tried to put in a story before. You never can tell.

Characterization can be made real by injecting bits of human behavior into the conduct and the actions of the individual you want to make impressive. Reactions, too, properly described, will do the job for you. When something dramatic happens in a story, don't let the character just stand there. Let her do something, say something, throw something -- react! Let her be alive!

The narrator must dominate the *action*, *generate real sympathy* on the part of the reader. Unsympathetic characters get nowhere in the Confessions. Once I tried being cleverly realistic by writing tough brittleness into a girl narrator's make-up. Back it came, with this comment, *"McLarn, don't you know any 'nice' ladies? This one is hard as a pool-ball. I want 'em sweet -- stupid, maybe, but sweet, dammit!"* And this came, too, *"It's impossible to like this screwball dame. And my readers wouldn't like her either. Quit trying to be so contemporary-slick, will ya?"*

Confessions are traditionally developed by a judicious blending of terse, realistic *dialogue* and *narration*, with emphasis on dialogue. But even dialogue can be overdone. A full column of yakking by one character gets pretty dull. Of course, long, dramatic speeches are sometimes essential to plot development and story line, but analysis of the pages of any Confession Book will show you that the longer speeches are broken every so often with stage directions, such as, "*He looked at me silently, as though he had never seen me before,*" or "*My fingers trembled as I lit a cigarette, smoked it half up before I could think of something to say.*" These little breaks in the action give the narrator and the reader time to collect their thoughts, and add to the suspense. They also give the writer a little time to think about what he's going to write next, too!

Editors get pretty sticky about the *ending of a tale.* In the slicks, endings can be vague, arty; leaving the reader to imagine what happens to the characters after THE END. But, to quote from the mast-head of one a few years back, "Confessions are Real Stories by Real People." The Real People who read Confessions don't get turned on by slickly artistic endings to their stories.

While some Confession writers are also slick-paper pros out for a quick buck, they're not supposed to let it show. Mary Rollins, once a top-flight Confession Editor, once told me, "McLarn, I could use more of your stuff, if you weren't so damned slick!"

When I get a script back with "Too fictional again, McLarn," scribbled on it, I do a fast re-write, and in my best pulp-paper style. Even if a story does have a 99-44/100% fiction aroma, if it doesn't have the *aura of reality* hanging over it, it won't get past the first reader in the Confession Shops. Be slick if you want to, but definitely not for the Confessions.

The third requirement of the Confession editors is a *consistent, emotional ending,* with no loose ends left fluttering in the breeze. The traditional ending of the Confession is usually the summing up of what the narrator has learned from the experience she has so graphically described to the reader; her final thoughts, shared by the reader, and in which the reader *could* believe. Religious endings are favorites of mine. I once concluded a tale about a man and a woman, two basically decent people who had drifted into a hopeless situation, and were about to pay a tragic price for their mistake, with this,

> "*We have done that which we should not have done; we have not done that which we should have done. Lord, have mercy upon us . . .*"

The editor wrote to thank me for my "realistic, dramatic ending." I wonder if he has since read the Book of Common Prayer.

I've ended many of my Confessions with a little prayer, the narrator's words trailing off into silence, indicated in the script by those handy five dots . . . . . "*. . . Please, God . . . . let me be worthy of this second chance to atone for my sin . . . .*" Corny? Sure. But isn't life pretty corny sometimes? And aren't Confessions stories about life as it really is?

I sometimes think that we "confessex writers" do not pay enough attention to what our editors say about "hope." One of my more somber efforts was returned with:

"Though her sins may be scarlet
And her loving not free
Let there be hope --
For her and for me . . ."

The editor said more in four lines than I could in four pages. I re-wrote the tale, sprinkling it liberally with the happy dust of "hope." Result, a nice sale. Why? Because I "Let There Be Hope" in the narrator's story; something that had been missing in the first version.

Go, and do thou likewise . . .

4 Confessions of a Confession Writer (Continued)

Interviewer: *Mr. McLarn, where do you get your ideas for Confessions? And does your wife know?*

I still have the same gorgeous wife I started out with, so I suppose that answers the first part of the question.

Where do Confession ideas come from? Not from personal research, that's for sure. But from just about every where else.

Confession ideas, plots, characters, situations are all around us. In newspaper articles, remarks overheard on a bus, from seemingly meaningless incidents that few people would even notice.

It is here that the writer's most important asset, imagination, comes into play. It is here that one single word starts the creative juices to flowing. The word *suppose*. Here's how it works:

The locale of the story-triggering incident is a high school parking lot, during a school dance. A boy and girl are standing beside the boy's car, talking. The boy obviously is trying to get the girl to leave the dance with him. She just as obviously doesn't want to go. He grabs her arm. She jerks away. He jumps into the car, sends it shrieking out of the parking lot.

The girl stares after him for a moment, tosses her head, goes back to the dance, alone.

Most people observing this little scene would shrug it off, saying, "*So what? They had a fight. He got mad and took off. Big deal!*" And forget all about it.

But this event contains a made-to-order idea for a teen-age Confession popular in many of the present crop of contemporary books. So let's apply our magic word to this situation, and see what happens.

Suppose — when the narrator tells the story, she reveals that what happened was the culmination of something that had been building up between the two young people for a long time.

Suppose — the narrator, frightened by what was stirring within her, told the boy that night that they had to "stop before it was too late."

Suppose — the boy, enraged because of her rejection of him, went charging off to the other side of town, where he picked up a more willing older girl, to salve his wounded ego in her arms and with her body.

Suppose — the next morning the narrator hears of her boy-friend and the other girl being found murdered on a lonely country road.

Finally, *suppose* that the narrator has such feelings of guilt and remorse because of her failure to realize the needs of her boy-friend that when she later falls in love and marries, on her wedding night she cannot respond physically or emotionally to the love-making of her new husband.

All this from just one brief scene, taking but a couple of minutes to play, which, by applying the *suppose* technique, became a salable 6,000 word Confession. All I did was back up a month or so, start the story at the beginning of the boy-girl thing, use the parking lot incident as the first climactic episode, and send the poor girl into marriage with a monumental psychological road-block for her to live with, to suffer with, and to eventually ovecome.

I won't tell you my version of how the girl solved her problem. I might want to use it again; it's a good old standard plot, with any number of possible solutions. But I will give you a hint. In my conclusion, the new husband was an understanding guy, and he did help -- a little. But not too much, for it is axiomatic that Confession narrators solve their own problems without extensive help from anybody. Except, maybe, God.

Yes, ideas are everywhere -- particularly in the advice columns of your own local newspapers. Some of the letters they publish provide excellent Confession material. One I used was from a girl whose own mother insisted that she take The Pill when she started going steady. The poor kid, hurt, bewildered, stunned by her mother's lack of trust, poured out her heartbreak to the sympathetic columnist.

I used the theme of the letter, but with my own twist. I had the boy-friend's mother give the girl a supply of the contraceptive, explaining to her that she didn't want her precious son to be "trapped into marriage," because she and her husband "had to get married" before the boy was born. I let the kids stumble along with the problem for a few thousand words, permitting them to *almost* go all the way, but finally had them decide on their own that they were mature enough and decent enough and loved each other enough to wait. I ended the story with them holding a gay little funeral ceremony, burying the preventives the boy's somewhat kooky mother had supplied.

Another story-producing letter was from a man whose doctor had pronounced him sterile, but his wife was pregnant. I wrote this one from the wife's viewpoint, stressing her agonized efforts to convince her husband that she hadn't cheated on him. The husband wanted to believe her, but couldn't cope with the situation. When the child was born, he was the spit-image of the husband, down to the same slightly malformed toe on his right foot! Clinch, forgive, curtain! (Naturally, I first got medical authority to confirm that certain types of male sterility aren't necessarily permanent.)

Editors are quite familiar with these sources. One wrote: "*Glad to know that you're a 'Dear Abby' reader, too. I'll get more on this one, but you seem to have come up first with what might be the best. Check coming.*"

The Confession Story must be a story that the reader can *believe in*. Not necessarily *believe*, but believe *in*. Or believe *could* have happened. Oh, sure -- the blurbs do say that Confessions are "Real Stories by Real People." But I know too many "Confessional Professionals" and I've seen too many of my own whole-cloth fabrications in print to be that naive. Maybe some of them are gospel, but, to quote from one of my favorite editors, "*Most we get are so lousy that we can't even read them, much less doctor them enough to use. We look to you 'old pros' to keep us and our readers happy.*"

At one time I spent a lot of effort on writing titles for my Confessions. No more. Not a single title I ever put on a Confession has ever been used with the published version. Now I use a working title -- one that doesn't give away too much of the story, but I don't waste much time on it. One editor told me that she would rather write her own titles, after consulting with the publisher's attorney and the advertisers, so she would have, "*Titles sexy enough on the covers to attract readers, but not so sexy as to get us in trouble with the law or the advertisers.*"

Speaking of titles, I've had editors call me long-distance and say something like, "*Look, McLarn, I've got to have six thousand words on I'M THE OFFICE SHE-WOLF! The front page is already set up with that title, we've got the illustrations, but no story! Get it to me come next Tuesday, sweetie! 'Bye!*"

When I get a call like that, I sit down and stare at the fiendishly grinning IBM Selectric keyboard for an hour or so, wondering how I ever got into such a cock-eyed business. But somehow the story gets written, by the dead-line, yet. Somehow. I guess that's why they call us "old pros." We get old before we're supposed to get old.

Interviewer: *Mr McLarn, how far will a Confession magazine permit you to go in telling a story?*
Me: *What you're really asking is, "Where does exciting, titillating writing end and pornography begin? When does the Confession Magazine move from the front of the book store or news stand to the curtained-off area where the 'hard core' stuff lurks?"*

That question has been asked in every interview I've given and at every seminar I've attended. It is still being asked everywhere magazines are on display for sale. A few years ago the campaign against "smut" was so intense in my home town that one drug-store chain succumbed to the alleged "public pressure" and barred all such publications from its stores. But the commercial magazine shops kept the Confessions right up front, among the standards, so apparently they weren't considered "pornos," in spite of the often lurid but just as often misleading story titles and cover illustrations. Even now, inside you don't always get what you see. Probably just as well, too. Anyway, the Confessions are back in those drug-stores. For now.

Some of today's paper-backs go far beyond anything the Confessions would dare publish. Just leafing through them sometimes gives me acute nausea. Descriptions of sex-activity, even downright perversion, in some of them would make Lady Chatterly resemble Elsie Dinsmore by comparison, and Fanny Hill read like the account of a knitting contest in an old ladies' home. Phew!

Confession editors are well aware of the campaigns against their publications. Some go to great lengths to keep their books out of the dirty class, stressing "decent realism." The word is that they are "Interested in good stories of the romantic type, with little or no sex." So they say. But one lady editor recently wrote me this:

"How much sex we like in a story, or how 'hot' the sex should be, depends on the story. With sexy, hot-blooded characters there can and should be some really sexy action. But of course in the present day our women readers still like to have love and romance along with their sex -- warmth, emotion, tenderness, and the like -- unless you're writing about a character who's not intended to be sympathetic, and is just out for all the sex he -- or she -- can get, without thinking of the other person's feelings or needs, sexual or otherwise.

"We know some of the Confessions are just interested in a good, hot, unusual sex situation, and the hell with logic or credibility. WE want everything! Good, believable, interesting stories that are sexy, too! We also buy stories that are simply romantic, with relatively little graphic sex."

A former editor on that same magazine once returned a script to me with, *"Another of 'McLarn's oversexed females!' Where do you find these (bleeps), anyway?"*

And from a relatively new Confession editor:

"How does an editor tell one of her favorite writers that she can't use his story? It isn't easy! This one is interesting, but definitely the kind of sexed-up story we do not run in our 'clean sex' publication. A friend does use really jazzy sex stories, so I'm passing your script on to her. I do hope she finds it acceptable. Don't get the idea that we're 'squeaky-clean' here. Our stories are loaded with sex, to be sure, but more believable sex, with strong reader identification . . ."

The second editor didn't buy the story, but the next one I sent it to did. After I made the sex more "believable." There's that word again!

In spite of the furor raised by the advocates of "clean literature," the Confessions are definitely not shying away from sex as such. They aren't cutting out the bedroom scenes. They still permit graphic descriptions of the reactions of both women and men to sexual stimulation and activity. But from the comments I receive and what I read, it is increasingly obvious that when sex scenes are used they must be in relatively good taste, and have definite bearing on the story -- not just dragged in for the purpose of adding sensationalism to an otherwise so-so yarn. Sex for sex's sake isn't enough. The story must come first -- and last, too.

Interviewer: *Mr. McLarn, what are your views on censorship? It seems that the Confessions would be the first targets of the censors.*
Me: *I try not to write anything so raw as to cloud anybody's mind or morals. After all, I do have grandchildren. But if some of the current movies, paper-backs, even TV, won't unglue the younger generation's sense of moral values, I doubt that the Confessions, the rather elemental stories about the gutsy side of life -- human error, human emotion, human suffering, human redemption, human — sometimes all too human — needs and desires -- will have all that much effect upon the decidedly hep young folks of today. And I think the reading, listening and viewing public is mature enough and sensible enough to decide what that public wants to read, hear and see, without the help from the professional do-gooders who seem to have appointed themselves guardians of our national morality. No, ma'am -- I do not like censorship. In ANY form.*

By a strange co-incidence, the day after I gave that interview, this came from the lady editor of a Confession book:

"By the way, we are going in for a pretty hot type of story now. Explicit sex, etc. Again -- keeping up with the times in the confessions . . ."

Here we go again.

If a story -- any story -- is properly written, submitted to the right market, at the right time, it will sell. If it isn't properly written, or goes to the wrong market, or to the right market at the wrong time, it won't. Editors are business people. For them to buy it, the product has to be right, has to meet a specific need, at the right time, and that's all there is to it.

The Confession section of WRITER'S MARKET and the various writing magazines will give you just about all the information you need to sell Confessions. But nothing will take the place of a patient, thorough, page-by-page analysis of the magazines themselves. Earlier in this treatise I mentioned that they may appear to be pretty much alike. But if you will write a one-page synopsis of a few stories in several different magazines, you will see that they are not alike -- in themes, situations, writing style, organization, even in "sexperiences." You'll find that one magazine will tell a story from beginning to end, in straight chronological order. Another will start the tale in the middle, with a highly sensational scene, then go into a long "flash-back," telling what happened before, what leads up to the opening scene, and then pick up the story and complete it. "Flash-back" is a good technique, but it's tricky. An editor fired a script back at me with, "*Fourteen pages of flash-back? McLarn, I ought to have my resident witch turn you back into a frog!*"

You will also find that where one magazine builds the reader up to fever-pitch, to where the sex action is about to ignite the bedding, and then cuts away to another unrelated bit of business, leaving the reader hanging, another will stay right with the reader, giving him a play-by-play account, escorting him, voyeur-like, through the whole bit, Alpha to Omega.

I am sometimes asked whether women narrators are more popular (meaning more salable) than men. Your research will tell you that women narrators outnumber men narrators about ten to one. I can, and often do, write from both viewpoints. But being a bit of a mercenary, I know that writing as a woman increases my chances of a first-submission sale; my highest word-rate comes from a magazine preferring women narrators, so I lean more and more to the female viewpoint. For a man my age to write as a teen-ager with a sex-problem does cause some eyebrow raising among "my public," but I "cry all the way to the bank."

> **Interviewer:** *You stepped on my next line. I was going to ask you how a grandfather, a senior citizen, with no formal training in writing, can turn out stories supposedly written by women or teen-age girls and make them sound convincing.*
> **Me:** *I wonder, too.*

I hadn't really thought about the question she raised. But in the answer is the whole basic idea of story-telling -- not just in Confessions, but in every area of writing.

Put this on the wall where you can see it every time you sit down at your typewriter:

The Only Way To Write A Convincing Piece Of Any Kind Is To Make Yourself A Part Of It.

Maybe I've learned that little trick -- with the help of the patient prodding of the Confession editors and a few others. Maybe I've learned how to become the character I'm writing about -- to get inside that character; think, talk, act, react as the character would, under the conditions I manufacture and the terms I set. Maybe I've learned how to become that teen-age girl with a sex hang up -- that truck driver with an unfaithful wife -- that policeman with a girl friend on the side -- that wife who is frigid with her husband and a push-over who has terrific orgasms with every other man on the block -- that man worried about youthful indiscretions that may be affecting his health, his job, his marriage, his manhood. Maybe I've learned to become that person vicariously -- and write as that person for as long as need be.

Maybe that's what psychologists call "role-playing." I don't know. But I do know that it works when I want it to work, and I can get up and walk away from it whenever I want to.

I can -- and frequently do -- become so emotionally involved in a story, with what happens to the people of my imagination, that I find myself weeping when my characters weep. And if a story makes its writer all that emotional, he can be pretty sure of the effect it will have on the reader. And, hopefully, on the editor first!

In a letter written just before her retirement, a veteran Confession editor summed up for me the whole principle of the Confessions when she wrote:

> *"One thing I stress again and again is that my readers want to believe that these stories are true. So I want stories that smack of the kitchen table. Sometimes we get one, seldom two from the same source, that I know to be the real thing . . .*
>
> *"Watch that tendency toward slick writing, Jack. The very qualified lead-ins to your stories always throw me. Of course, that's the way a story should start -- but it ain't the real Confession thing, baby -- not by a long shot! Your lead-ins are the mark of a craftsman. Want a suggestion? Write your lead -- then scratch it, and really start your story with paragraph two! In that way you avoid the fatal hazard of being 'slick' -- of being a good writer. Our readers wouldn't know a well-written, well done story from a crepe suzette! They want scandal, they want romance, they want to weep, weep, weep. You should see the letters I get when we print a particularly sloppy story! They say, 'I cried all night! Thank you for the most beautiful story I ever read!' Boy, do they like to* suffer*!"*

Who wouldn't treasure a letter like that? I miss her breezy, salty commentaries tremendously. I never met her, but I know she has been just as kind and just as helpful to a lot of other writers such as this one. She just couldn't help it!

Probably the most interesting and intriguing rejection slip I ever received, from a Confession editor or anyone else, consisted of a single incomplete sentence -- "*Meanwhile, back at the ranch . . .*" That was all.

After I got to know the rejecting editor a little better, I asked her what she meant by that cryptic attachment to my rejection script. Her reply was:

> "*Sometimes an editor gets a story that seems to have all the essentials, but it still just doesn't feel right. I don't like printed rejection slips, and I hate to do what some of my associates do -- send the story back without anything with it -- guess I'm too tender-hearted -- so I just put down something. And sometimes it makes sense. I remember your story that drew that crack. It was just too ho-hum! In other words -- blaahhh!*"

I once sent another editor two stories in the same envelope. Back they came, with this blast:

> "*One at a time, okay? But no sale, anyway.*
>
> "*My readers want narrators they can like. So do I. But who could like these two characters? The way you draw them, they're just a couple of sobbing losers with whom life has dealt harshly -- and they don't do a durned thing about it! Surely they could try to help themselves, even if what they do is completely stupid, gosh-awful wrong, and louses things up worse than ever.*
>
> "*When you start playing God with that typewriter, let your characters get off their cans and at least try to change things -- perhaps by getting rid of the hang-ups they have allowed to dominate their lives -- maybe by doing some realistic self-evaluation, resulting in some kind of positive action.*
>
> "*And while I'm in this helpful mood, I wish you'd quit sending me these gosh-awful 'hopeless ending' scripts. I get the feeling that you don't like them any more than I do -- and I sure don't. Cheer up -- things aren't all that bad!*"

I rewrote both tales. One sold. I'm still trying to sell the other.

One of the long-time guiding geniuses of the Confessions answered my somewhat naive question as to his needs in this characteristic fashion:

> *"Oh, Lord, McLarn -- you too? I always hate to sit down and try to write out what we look for. It's all been said so often by so many, but I'll try.*
>
> *"We want characters, especially narrators, that a reader can care about, get involved with emotionally. Real people, not just cardboard cut-outs. Something happening, and not just 'sin-suffer-repent'. Preferably a viable, living 'Confession' angle -- but not necessarily, if the story is otherwise strong. Without the Confession angle, however, a story does tend to lack a theme. Some element of freshness, which could be provided by timelessness. For instance, a few years ago you couldn't have written a story about a college campus rebellion. There weren't any. Then the riots. Now -- calm again. Things change. So do our stories. We want stories to keep the reader reading, absorbed, to the end -- which the reader is sorry to see come . . ."*

He too, is enjoying his retirement, just as I am enjoying my own. Confessions will never be the same without him.

"*Suppose*" we conclude this chapter with a few random observations about this fascinating Confession medium.

Take a look about you. Don't you know of someone -- even yourself -- who would make a good Confession Writer? Someone with a "secret" that would make a good Confession? If it could be told?

Okay, let's talk about you. Surely you must recall an incident in your own life that would provide a theme for a Confession. Why not get it off your chest -- or your conscience -- under the forever inviolate anonymity of the Confessions? Or why not rub your own personal Aladdin's Lamp, summon your own personal *jinni,* the *jinni* of imagination; say to him, "*Suppose, jinni!*", and take it from there. You are a writer, else you would never have read this far in this book. And a writer is trained to think, not of things as they are, but as what he wills them to be.

Having done all this, you won't need me or anybody else to tell you what to write, or how to write it. Your narrator will take over for you, live her mistakes, suffer for them. But in the end she will solve her problems, whatever they are, and find her own way out.

Don't let yourself intrude. Don't let yourself try for literary excellence. Just let your narrator be a human being. Here is a device I often use. I visualize my narrator sitting in a third-floor walk-up, at a kitchen table, writing on tablet paper -- garbage and soiled diapers reeking under the sink -- the people downstairs throwing things and screeching at each other. With maybe a baby crying in the next room (or dying). More often than not, I'm right there, too.

Write it just as you "*suppose*" it could have happened. Mail it to one of the Confessions. You might sell it. You might get it back, too. So what? If it does come back, don't start a by-mail argument with the editor. Editors are notoriously right. If you do sell it, you won't get a by-line, and unless you want to reveal your authorship yourself -- which you probably will -- your Confession will remain your secret, forever and amen.

If you take my gratuitous advice and try a Confession, and some editor buys it and rejects one of mine it'll be because yours is better. And I'll be delighted. Well, sort of, anyway.

Interviewer: *Mr. McLarn, you write other things besides Confessions now, don't you? Does that mean you're trying to "live down" your reputation as a ?—."*
Me: *As a Confession writer? No, indeed. I'm trying to live up to it!*

I do have a lot to live up to. Much of whatever writing ability I have, in and out of the confession field, I acquired through my association with a handful of the most knowledgeable editors in the business. From them I learned how to plot, how to develop a story, how to write convincing dialogue, how to do just about everything that a writer does. They were tough, but they were fair -- and I still feel that they mean it when they say, as one lady editor did recently, "Jack, I'm glad I could buy this story."

So I conclude this chapter with a personal word to any of My Friends, the Confession Editors who might read this book.

"Thanks, ladies and gentlemen of 'Sin, Suffer and Repent,' for what you have done to make me whatever I am in the literary field. H'its been pleasurable. I've had myself a ball. . ."

5 Business and Educational Writing

Interviewer: *Mr. McLarn, let's talk about your other writing activities. For instance, what's this I hear about your being known in some areas as a "business and educational writer"?*

Me: *Yes, I do some writing in the business and educational field. And if you want a definition of a business-dash-educational writer, I can't think of a better one than that given by a charming lady who has close to a thousand articles to her credit: "To be a business-educational writer, you have to know or find out more about your subject than anybody else, and put it down on paper before you forget it."*

In writing fiction, the writer has no confines, no limits, other than those of his imagination. He can indulge in flights of fancy, changes of locale, quirks of character, and if he slips up somewhere, chances are the reader will not even notice it. After all, fiction is for entertainment, not for education.

But when that same writer abandons the never-never land of his imagination, and decides to do some fact writing, he enters the grim, harsh world of reality, where he must know whereof he writes.

This was brought home to me with a bang some years ago, when the editor of a trucking company "House Organ" asked me to write an article publicizing a new long-distance schedule the line was inaugurating. He gave me a lot of material to read; I absorbed it, banged out the article in a couple of evenings, congratulating myself on the ease with which my prose flowed from my brain into my fingers into my typewriter.

When the editor finished reading my neatly typed script, I found that trucking company vernacular was just as rough as railroad lingo. Somewhat expurgated, his comments were to the effect that if he published the craapola I had ground out, everybody would know that I had never seen the cab of a diesel tractor-trailer combination, and both of us would be laughed out of the industry.

"McLarn," he said. "This would be good if you were writing the stuff I hear you specialize in. But, mister, you're dealing with facts now. For God's sake go get some facts, and try again."

When he finally cooled down, he arranged for me to make a run with a diesel jockey on the schedule he was trying to publicize. Considerably chastened, I took a week-end off, climbed into the cab of a semi, prepared to have the daylights scared out of me.

It took three days. Three days in the cab of the semi, with a long-haired, beady eyed, bearded young driver who took no pains at all to hide his contempt for his cab-mate. The first hundred miles were spent in silence. But he was a nice guy, and he eventually thawed. By the time we finished the round trip, we had become friends -- and I knew things about trucking that gave me a completely new viewpoint. And I finally got through my head the incredibly complex gear-shifting that was routine to my companion. The way he tooled the massive rig over the hair-raising highways of the Blue Ridge, the way he maneuvered the box-car sized trailer into an unloading dock barely inches wider than itself, the way he and his fellow truckers used their "citizen's band" radios to warn of hazards -- including highway patrol officers on the lookout for overloads and speeders -- gave me more information than I could possibly use.

Back at my typewriter, the article fairly flowed. But when I read it over, I got a shock. It wasn't me. It was my young diesel jockey. It was his story. True, the words were mine, but the spirit was his.

I took it to the editor. He fairly beamed. "Boy, you did it," he said. "You sound as though you had driven a semi for years. I'll get you your check."

"No," I said. "I'm just the reporter. Put that kid's by-line on it. It's his."

We finally compromised on using the kid's by-line, with "as-told-to" me, and we each took half the money. Maybe I didn't do him any favor by getting him "noticed." When the story came out, his company yanked him out of his beloved diesel cab and put him on a desk job -- an "executive," yet. He could still wear his hair long, but without the beard. Too bad -- on him it looked good. It was saddening to learn that he finally quit, joined the army. He was one of the ones who didn't make it back from 'Nam.

That experience convinced me that just about everybody has something inside him that needs to be brought out. I brought an ability out of him -- just as knowing him brought an ability out of me -- the ability to take what a man says, or doesn't say, and put it down on paper. Convincingly.

I guess that's why I got involved in writing, while making my living doing something else. Because I had something to say, even if somebody else helped me say it. I believe everybody has something to share. One field of sharing is that of Business and Educational Writing.

The Business Writer

The one greatest business problem today is that of "Communication." There was a time when sketchy, incomplete data or direction showed up in an operation, it would only result in a minor foul-up. There were enough checks and balances along the way to insure detection and correction of the defective procedure or method before too much went wrong

But with today's high-speed computers, instantaneous transmission of intelligence, the very speed of action to which modern business is geared can result in drastic consequences, simply because there is so little time between the initiating and accomplishment of an endeavor for building in safeguards against error. It is because of this very quirk of modern living that it is so vital that communication of any kind be rapid, readily understandable, and impeccably correct.

As a Departmental Manager, one of my responsibilities was to interview prospective employees in a highly technical area. Applicants ranged from high school and business school graduates, degree-bearing college graduates, even retired military officers and personnel. I was surprised to find that the one almost universal characteristic among the dozens of people interviewed, of varying ages and economic status, was unwillingness to accept the fact that a basic industry is the need for the ability to communicate effectively -- not only the ability to impart information and direction quickly and accurately, but to receive and understand that information, counsel, direction, just as quickly and just as accurately.

Managers have long recognized this problem. But any manager in any business has a complex, frustrating job. He knows what should be done, but rarely has the time, few have the qualifications, and even fewer the patience and the temperament to sit down and do the tedious, exacting job of spelling out the detail involved, the knowledge that must be imparted, the training that must be undertaken, and the end result that must be accomplished. It is then that the Business Writer comes into the picture. Usually a bit late, but eventually he does come.

In the segment of the industry in which I spent my entire

working life, it suddenly become necessary that the craftsperson in the area of equipment maintenance become familiar with a new set of " rules" governing how work was to be done, and a new manner of reporting the performance of that work.

Rules pertaining to the work itself had existed for years -- but in a form and language beyond the grasp of the workmen, skilled though they were in the mechanics of doing that work. They did their jobs; they made the repairs in conformance with those rules; but only because they knew vaguely that "it had to be done that way," but didn't quite know why.

To borrow from Bret Harte, the "ways of corporations are peculiar." A complete stranger to the operation, I was summarily taken from my comfortable routine job, and assigned to putting the complex, often ambiguous wordage of the long extant "rules" into what amounted to another language -- into the day-to-day communication among the workmen, and between them and their supervisors.

Overnight I had to become a Business Writer -- and in a field about which I new next to nothing.

My first impulse was to hole up with that ancient "Rule Book" and a typewriter, and convert the archaic language into modern day idiom. But when I remembered my fiasco with the diesel-driving article, I changed my mind. There was but one thing to do -- get the facts. There was but one way to do that. It amounted to me, a white-collar front office man, qualifying myself as a tool-using craftsperson.

For weeks I literally lived with the workmen and their supervisors, doing things wrong that even the greenest apprentice did right. When the craftsmen themselves got over their suspicion of the "front office stiff" with the new coveralls in their midst, they played enough in-house tricks on me to last quite a while.

I studied by night, often falling asleep with my glasses on and my "rule book" on my chest. I worked along with the craftsmen by day, learning by listening to them, learning by doing, trying to duplicate the expertise of the amused and not overly co-operative craftsmen. Gradually, I began to understand what they did, and just as gradually I began to put into every-day words a combination of what "the rules" required, and what the craftsmen did. It took weeks of writing, revising and writing again to finally develop a manual that brought together the technical and the practical aspects of the maintenance of equipment operation. That manual was used for years. It has now been replaced by a computerized system, one that leaves nothing to chance, but my manual was the first -- and last -- of its kind. At least I have that to remember!

The job of the Business Writer is to put into readily understandable words step-by-step procedures, often developed by trial-and-error, for solving problems -- plant and office layouts, material or paper-handling routines, personnel or administrative complications, or, as in the case of my diesel jockey friend, finding a better way of teaching drivers to tool their tons of controlled fury over mountains and through valleys. It is the Business Writers who put complicated theory into simplified routine; who reduce the details of "problem solving" to a minimum of understandable wordage, a maximum of terse directness, and a whole lot of understanding. The only way they do this effectively is by first knowing what they intend to do, finding how it is done now, and determining how to do it from now on. And that cannot be done by reading a few books and sitting down before a typewriter.

Sure, I got paid for writing my "manual." It was part of my regular job. But I didn't expect the payment that came in the form of a letter.

> *"Mr. McLarn, we would like to congratulate you, and say a hearty 'well done!' for the new billing manual. It is the most complete source of information of its kind in the industry. It appears that you have eliminated practically all chance of mistake. For the Division -- congratulations, and thanks for a job well done."*

It was signed by every member of the repair force at one of the maintenance points -- the same characters whose idea of a joke was to slip up behind me and drop a white-hot rivet in the back pocket of my coveralls. Of course, the rivet burned right through to the ground, but its passage down my leg was sufficiently torrid to make itself felt, to the delight of my tormentors. I still have that letter. And I still get a warm glow of satisfaction every time I run across it. In the industry in which I spent my whole working life, there is nothing more rewarding to a front office person to have craftspeople admit that he knows the difference between the A-end and the B-end of a box car!

I know of no magic formula that will help a writer gain entry into the field of Business Writing, except that it helps to have or develop a certain ability to gather facts, and to present those facts in a new setting. I once found in my mail box a brochure describing a new apartment complex being rented. The art work was superb, but the accompanying description was as dull as yesterday's pizza.

Out of curiosity, I drove to the complex, convinced the security guard that I wasn't there to rip off the place, and strolled through. I was impressed with the design, the arrangement, the grounds, and the kind of people who were also looking the apartments over. A couple of days later, I rewrote the brochure, eliminating most of the correctly written but stuffy descriptive material, and mailed my version, along with my card, to the realty firm renting the apartments. Two weeks later I received another brochure, with the same art work, but with my material -- along with a note thanking me for my interest in the complex, and complimenting me on my brochure writing ability.

Three months later, the president of that same realty firm commissioned me to write a sales training course for their sales staff, using material that had been accumulated over the years.

"You take my stuff," he said. "And put it into the kind of words you wrote into that brochure."

The whole premise behind Business Writing is the same as there is behind salesmanship. The salespersons sense that a person, client, or prospect has a problem. The salespersons find out what that problem is, and use their sales know-how to solve it. The Business Writer does exactly the same thing -- finds the problem, develops the solution, and delivers that solution to where it will do the most good.

But it isn't enough to just "develop" the solution. The solution has to apply to the immediate problem. Even if you have the answer, that answer must be couched in the language, the idioms of the problem.

The first thing that needs to be done is to look about you, in your community, and select the field of endeavor at which you want your efforts to be aimed. Almost every industry has its own "House Organ," its own "News Letter." When you select your target, get whatever information you can about the specific industry or firm. When you do your writing, make sure that the language you use is the same as that used in the company publication. Literally put yourself into the plant, the factory, the material yard, just as though you actually worked there every day.

Just about every industry belongs to some sort of a Trade Association. If you find the one your target company belongs to, send a brief letter to the director of the Association, outlining your idea of doing some writing for the firms in the group, and ask that your name be mentioned to the various industries as being a Business Writer, available for publicity and in-house writing. If you get no response, try another field. It won't be exactly earth-shaking, but you should get some response. Keep trying -- if it worked for me, it will work for you, too. Get one writing assignment, and if you do the kind of job the firm wants, you'll get more.

6 Business and Educational Writing (Continued)

Interviewer: *Mr. McLarn, how does an admittedly self-educated man compete with the PhD's and others who write educational material?*
Me: *I don't try to "compete" with them. The kind of educational writing I do doesn't appeal to the majority of the text-book writers, because it's just plain hard work. But for me it has a certain satisfaction. I like to think what I do in the field just might help somebody select his career.*

I'm gun-shy whenever somebody mentions "education" in my presence. Most people have far more of that invaluable asset than I do. The only degrees I have are those found on a thermometer when my temperature goes haywire, and the mere presence of an MA, PhD, PhiBeta, BS, or even a "fraternity man" reduces me to complete, tongue-tied silence.

"Educational Writing" makes most folks think of text books, usually written to order for publishers by college professors -- who promptly make their books required texts for their courses, thereby increasing their royalties -- or by moonlighting teachers, so the field is a rather limited one. However, I stumbled onto at least one area of Educational Writing in which even the part-timer can do pretty well, and derive a whole lot of satisfaction from it, too.

Some years ago, one of the writing magazines ran an advertisement for a New York State concern that wanted writers to prepare "Occupational Briefs." Being an inveterate ad-answerer, and not knowing what an "Occupational Brief" was, I responded. The reply included this:

> "*Occupational briefs are one type of written occupational literature used by students investigating occupations. While sound occupational choice is a result of many factors, appropriately prepared occupational information can serve an important purpose by providing students with general background information, specific information on educational training requirements, and sources of additional information.*
>
> "*Our briefs are designed to provide counsellors, teachers, and high school students with an objective over-view of a specific occupational area.*"

The charming Research Assistant went on to say that the information should be of immediate practical value to both the job-or-college-bound student; that the material should be prepared to help students plan the specific steps they should consider next, to enter the occupation being described.

She said that the briefs should contain a "*clear statement of the abilities and the interests related to the occupation and the educational and/or training requirements; hobbies, as a reflection of interests; special skills or abilities as an indication of aptitudes; accomplishment in specific high school courses as an indication of academic aptitude; specific high school programs required for admission to post-high school training . . . The author should strive to present a concise, accurate, balanced, unbiased and factual overview of the occupational area . . .*"

She concluded by saying that whatever I wrote would be passed upon by about seven authorities in the field covered, three of whom would have to approve what I said before the script would be accepted. Now, with all that in mind, since I had spent my life in the railroad industry, would I please write for her an "Occupational Brief" on the "Railroad Transportation Industry?" Twelve typewritten pages. Three thousand words, double-spaced. She enclosed a very detailed statement of the points she wanted, a list of "possible sources of information" as long as my arm, and a postage-paid return envelope.

My first impulse was to tell the lady that putting the "Railroad Transportation Industry" into three thousand words, double-spaced, was comparable to putting the Book of Genesis on the head of a pin. But I wrote the brief -- and was startled to know how little I really knew about the industry in which I had literally lived for so long. But I kept at it, researching, studying, remembering, consulting the "guide-lines" the lady had sent me, until I had covered, in high-school language, such things as the history of the industry, some of the kinds of work performed, the working conditions employees of various types might expect, the high school courses one should take to prepare for specific areas of railroading; what personal qualifications one should have; how to apply for employment; advancement or promotional possibilities, employment outlook; approximate earnings; social and psychological factors -- work satisfaction, relationship with people, union requirements -- the list went on and on, and I had to condense and condense, to stay within my three thousand word confines.

With misgivings, I mailed the script to the lady. Weeks passed, and I had all but written the thing off as a bad job, when she wrote that the script had been reveiwed and accepted, and here was my check. Several months later I received copies of the printed brief, and was surprised to read that some of the reviewers of the document were associates of mine on railroads other than my own. They'll probably never know that I wrote the script as Occupational Briefs do not carry the by-line of the writer. But there was a warm glow of satisfaction all over me as I read what I had written. That glow was enhanced when the publisher sent me a letter from a kid in the mid-west, wanting to know more about "how to be a railroad man" . . . .

Since my introduction to this highly specialized area of Educational Writing, the publisher has called on me a couple of times each year, to produce briefs on such occupations as Freight Traffic Consultant, Safety Engineer, Industrial Hygienist, Harbor Master, Memorial Designer, and, for this year, I've just begun the research into the occupations of Mobile Home Repairer and (!) Sewage Plant Operator/Attendant!

The brief I remember most pleasantly is the one on the Mining and Quarrying Industry. That one was tough. I get claustrophobia in a Pullman car roomette with the door closed, so the thought of going underground to do research on this project was downright terrifying. But I did it, and with the help of the Bureau of Mines, the United Mine Workers, the Coal Institute, the Department of Labor Dictionary of Occupational Titles, the Occupational Outlook Handbook, and a couple of encyclopedias, I finally finished it, with no more than a few bruises from not ducking low enough entering a mine "room," but with a whole lot of respect and admiration for the men who go down into the earth to bring out the black energy we call coal. I was elated to hear, months later, that the publisher had been awarded a plaque for the brief on Mining and Quarrying.

Occupational Brief writing isn't an easy way to make money. It takes a tremendous amount of research, and a lot of re-writing. The researchers on the publisher's staff are so knowledgeable that I often wonder why they don't do the briefs themselves, instead of paying me five cents a word. But as long as the ladies call on me, I'll respond. Five cents a word won't buy a new car every year, but will sure buy the gas to run the ancient one I drive!

To me, at least, Occupational Brief writing is one of the most rewarding things I do. I have the feeling that maybe I'm sharing something rather special with the young people who might find a career because of my research and my writing. Of course, I'll never know. But I wish my high school English teacher could know that I write these briefs. She told me that I should *"never get into any vocation that would make any form of self-expression necessary . . . You just don't have the knack for it!"*

> **Interviewer:** *Mr. McLarn, I notice you're taping this interview. Have you ever thought of writing audio-visual material?*
> **Me:** *Yes. But sometimes I wonder why!*

Oh, sure. According to all the writing books, Audios and Ausio-Visuals constitute another rapidly growing area of Educational Writing.

The "Audio" aspect consists of tape recordings on reels or cassettes, used in relatively inexpensive recording and play-back machines. Originally these tapes were used for training sales and management personnel, the material being house-written and put on tapes by recording companies equipped to professionally record and duplicate the lectures, courses, etc. Now it has become big business, with producers buying scripts on many subjects -- salesmanship, management training, how to speak a foreign language, how to learn the Morse code -- even how to write short stories! Some publishers are putting standard text books on cassettes; others put children's stories out in cassette form. The definitive book, WRITER'S MARKET, devotes an entire section to this market -- types of material wanted, payment to be expected, and the like.

Yes, I tried the field. By answering an advertisement in the "Writers Wanted" section of a writing magazine. The mid-western publisher sent me a whole list of suggested programs on various phases of "Management Training," invited me to take my pick, write a one-hour program -- eight thousand words -- in the format he suggested. He even sent me a pair of cassettes, illustrating what he wanted.

Years before, I had written some short radio plays for a 100-watter in the Deep South, for free. I pretended I was writing a radio script, did my 8,000 words on "Concepts of Management," sent it off, fully expecting to get a "sorry, but . . ." brush-off. Instead I received a whopping check, and an enthusiastic request to do another program! I did the second one, got the same big check!

Elated, I shopped around for more outlets for my newly acquired product. Another ad appeared in that same writer's magazine, wanting "Cassette Writers." Again I answered. Again I got an assignment – this time on a formal contract, with a royalty that made my eyes pop. This time the deal was for me to write the script for an entire course! I wrote the script. It was produced, and superbly. I visited the offices of the firm. They were plush; the equipment was the best money could buy; the officers were charmingly affable -- so much so that I didn't think I'd need a lawyer to look over the contract. Then, as I mentioned in Chapter II of this opus, the roof fell on me. The firm suddenly went broke; the Sales Manager acquired it, and wrote me that " . . . Unfortunately for you Mr. McLarn, I bought only the assets of the company, not the liabilities. Sorry."

Only then did I call my lawyer. Too late.

Later, to "make it up to me," the new owner of the business commissioned me to do another series for him. This time I was smart enough to get an advance. I produced a script, he had it recorded, it sold all over the country. But when I tried to collect the rest of my fee, you guess what happened. "Gone -- no forwarding address."

"Pretty stupid," said My Friend, My Lawyer. You should never enter into any kind of a contract without getting legal advice. I would have never let you get yourself into that kind of a mess. I would have insisted that the material be copyrighted in your name; that if the company went out of business, all rights would revert to you, and a lot of other things your contract doesn't contain, including royalty payments every six months. I would try, even this late, to get the master tapes back. But if the guy's smart, he's already sold them, and you're left holding the well-known bag."

Why do I continue to wear a hair shirt because of this fiasco? To put across one point. I'm sure you know what it is.

So cassette writing is a sore spot with me. But we live and learn. Since then I've had inquiries from a firm on the West Coast about doing some short scripts for them, at a flat fee. Four have been produced, and paid for, so far. A Chicago publisher suggested that I record a script myself and send him the cassette. I did, but I'm afraid my Nawth Ca'lina drawl won't do much for the cassette industry, although I do have hopes. Another publisher wanted to know if I edited books and other material down to one-hour cassettes. I'm still trying to decide what to tell him. Probably no . . .

Some cassette publishers pay on a per-word or per-recorded hour basis. Others pay royalties. They are all very specialized as to their wants; it would be inadvisable to spend the time and effort a "speculative" script would require. But it is an interesting and potentially profitable field, and if you have a flair for dialogue, and the patience to do a lot of research, inquiries addressed to several of the cassette producers in WRITER'S MARKET might get you an assignment. I wish you better luck than I had.

As to "Audio-Visuals," they are sophisticated film-and-sound packages, produced about the same as a slick TV show. The scripts are prepared with the same care as are scripts for TV productions. I flopped in this medium. I could write the "Audio" portion, but when I tried the "Video," my script was returned with: *"Sorry -- the Audio we might use, but not the video . . ."*

Many of the Audio-Visual producers use only their own staff writers. If you must try them, I again refer you to WRITER'S MARKET. Lots of luck.

I haven't tried to cover all the opportunities in Business and Educational Writing. The part-timer doesn't have the hours to spend on something that might not pay off. But there are a few more possibilities worth considering.

Book reviewing, for one. I built up quite a library for my daughter by reviewing books for local newspapers -- my fee being that I got to keep the book.

Term papers for college students -- confined to helping the student organize his material, putting it in shape for typing, but NOT doing his paper for him. I've had requests for that sort of thing, and I know a few people who do it, but it's not for me. Even if I could, I wouldn't.

Executives, politicians and others are good prospects for "ghost written" speeches, lectures, seminar papers, even novels. I did a lot of this for my company officers while I was working, and rightly so. They didn't have the time. I did. Now I do it -- the difference being that I get paid for it. So can you.

No matter what your background is, you can be pretty sure that somewhere there is a magazine devoted to that background. There are dozens of house organs and magazines that specialize in particular industries, especially your own. Ten to one you'll one day realize that you, too, have something to say about the company you work for, own stock in, or know something about. You'll not only have fun, but you might get paid for it -- start a whole new thing for yourself!

The field of Business and Educational Writing is not easy to crack -- nor is it always financially rewarding. I'm still stuck with a script I labored over for six months, titled "Constructive Salesmanship," which several cassette publishers have pronounced interesting, but, as one of them put it, "McLarn, 'Sales Training' has been flogged to death. Give us something new."

And another cassette publisher came up with his lament:

> "*It appears that one of the major reasons that the marketing of cassettes always seems to be a disappointment is that there is significant unauthorized copying and this eliminates the most profitable part of the business -- referrals by satisfied customers. Further, it almost completely elim-*

inates sales by direct mail. We think that we would have a different situation entirely if this problem could be solved.

Discouraging? Yes. But realistic.

Yet, reverting to my former theme, there are rewards to this kind of writing that cannot be put in the bank, but cannot be discounted, either. Such as a note from a book author, written at his exotic island home, thanking me for "... understanding what I was trying to say. Your review had the ring of honesty ... I think you actually read the book!"

A note from a Sales Manager, telling me of using one of my articles in his sales lectures, because it "... gives the viewpoint of somebody who has been through the mill ..." And learning from a retail store owner that my cassette course in retailing was so effective that one of his least productive salesmen had become one of his best! I never got paid a dime for that course ... yet I feel somehow rewarded for having produced it.

A boy writing me that because of one of my Occupational Briefs, the industry I analyzed was going to be his own life's work.

And finally, one of my own former subordinates sending me a Christmas card, thanking me for " . . .what you tried to tell us about getting along with people . . ."

He got my job when I retired.

7 Writing for Children—and Kids

> **Interviewer:** *Mr. McLarn, how does a man your age, known for writing some pretty hot adult fiction, manage to write convincingly for children?*
>
> **Me:** *I don't write for "children." I write for "kids."*

To me, "children" are shining-scrubbed, prim-starched little girls; highly polished little boys uncomfortable in shorts and blouses a size too large, playing silly party games, supervised by beamingly approving, but "don't-you-dare-get-dirty!" mammas. They have an unreality about them that I have never been able to authentically depict.

But "kids" are dirty-faced, noisy, uninhibited youngsters who splash happily in mud-puddles, climb forbidden trees, dig in off-limits ditches for creepy-crawly things to bring home. They are grubby little girls, grubbier little boys, playing their improvised games, sharing their "secrets," with no thought of the built-in differences that will one day set them apart — and another day bring them even closer together.

These are the kids I learned to "tell 'tories to" so long ago. I never did look upon them as children. Not then. Certainly not now, either.

Writing for kids is a Very Special Art, if not a Gift. Writing for an adult audience, the writer can and must concentrate on such technicalities as plot structure, style, qualified lead-in, surprise twists -- all the classic devices so dear to the hearts of creative writers that show off their super-craftsmanship, without having to pay too much attention to such minor considerations as approved vocabularies, basal reading, graded word-lists, attention span, and the thinking level of their audience. After all, adult writers know they are writing for their peers, and that if their readers have bat-brains they will know what they are trying to say, no matter if they use five-syllable words of doubtful meaning, and wallow through every one of Mister Polti's Thirty-Six Dramatic Situations -- or are there thirty-seven?

When those same writers turn out one of those Little Stories for Little Folks, however, it doesn't take them long to find that not only are they in a whole new ball game; they are in one where they can get knocked out of the box in the first inning -- not by the antiseptically cotton-wool encased, squeaky-clean "children," but by the runny-nosed, dirty-faced, skinned-kneed kids into which children somehow manage to develop when their fond parents are looking the other way.

Any writer who thinks that in writing for children he has found a cushy way of making money has quite a surprise awaiting.

Writing for kids, as opposed to writing for children, is one of the most complex undertakings a writer ever faces. Kids' tastes, their viewpoints, their vocabularies, even their thinking processes, change rapidly and erratically, year to year, month to month, even day to day. They change in the "to-be-read-to" group, in the "just-learning-to-read" set, the "first-reader" types, the "go-to-the-library-by-myself-and-get-a-book" level achievers. They change within mighty short age-spans, too -- and the writer who sends a six-year-old-type story to a book that courts nine-year-old readers is inviting a fast rejection.

WRITER'S MARKET has recognized this. The juvenile section of the book is headed with a list of juvenile publications classified by age groups, thus saving us many hours of research, as well as quite a bit of postage, by channeling our efforts in the right direction at the beginning, instead of letting us find out the hard way.

Kids want to read about kids like themselves, and just like themselves. And the writer who would write for kids has to learn how to use the oldest writing gimmick of all. To write for kids, they must become the kid they are writing about, and the kids they are writing for. They must think as the kids think, reason as the kids reason, act -- and react -- as the kids act and react. And finally realize and themselves experience the kind of reward the kids would want to enjoy.

Years ago, I had the best of all possible teachers in writing for kids. My own small daughter was never a *child*, but always a *kid*. In many ways she is still a *kid* today, along with her own three teen-agers.

When she was very young, I had to travel extensively, often being away from home a week at a time. During my absences, she naturally had her mother's full time attention, and I was little more than a name, a voice on a telephone, a shadowy somebody "away somewhere on a train." Consequently, when I did come home, she didn't have monopoly of her mother. That snub nose would go out of joint, that lower lip would acquire a permanent curl, and often her very first words to me were, "Hi, daddy. When you go 'way 'gain?"

The blunt honesty of a kid can be pretty abrasive, even to a hard-nosed railroad man. My small daughter's "welcome away" hit pretty hard. So hard as to give both her mother and me concern. We soon realized that I had better do something to enhance my status with my tiny, outspoken little daughter. So one night, when she was being more defiantly reluctant to go to bed than usual, I had a sudden inspiration.

"Honey," I said. "Let daddy put you to bed, and he'll tell you a story, okay?"

She regarded me levelly for a full minute, obviously having an enthusiastic lack of interest in the idea. But it was something new, so she allowed me to tuck her in. It was that night I became a kids' story-teller.

Where I got the character I'll never know, but from somewhere in my imagination came Oomyak the Eskimo. Oomyak, and his dog, a huge Alaskan husky, Kayak.

I'll always remember that night. The look on my daughter's pixie face, her corn-flower eyes fixed unwaveringly upon mine, a new light glowing in them as I floundered through my tale -- and it was a dilly! About the frozen northland, the icy tundra, the stunted pine trees. About a little boy her age, scolded by his parents, running away from his igloo, his snow-block home, with faithful Kayak plowing through the deep snow beside him. The two of them, alone, frightened, cold, wandering in the Arctic night, with the Northern Lights flickering endlessly in the sky.

When I paused, having gotten the little boy and the great dog hopelessly lost in the frozen wastes, there were tears in my little girl's eyes.

"Please, daddy!" she quavered. "Don't let them stay out in the cold! Please let them come home!"

It was then that I realized what had happened. I had accomplished something that many writers never do. I had convinced the most critical of all audiences that my story was a story a kid could believe!

Happily, I brought Oomyak and Kayak home to their snow-block house. And when they were all safe and warm among Oomyak's numerous brothers and sisters in the smoky igloo, my daughter breathed a shaky sigh of relief.

"Daddy, that was the goodest 'tory I ever heard in my whole life!" she said. She reached up, pulled my head down, kissed me smackingly good-night voluntarily for the first time in weeks. "Now, say my prayers wif' me, okay?"

That did it. From then on, I was welcomed home with glowing enthusiasm and wet kisses. There was never a problem about bed-time, for that meant a new "'tory" about Oomyak and Kayak. And I always delivered.

I read so much about Eskimos and Alaska and Labrador and the Midnight Sun that my wife threatened to feed me seal meat, with whale blubber for dessert. But I had to keep my tales authentic, for I had a pretty sharp little audience. I learned to detect the slightest flicker of questioning disbelief in my daughter's face, the faintest sign of wandering attention, and I made sure that it didn't happen as I told the next "'tory."

That went on for months -- old stories, repeated stories, new stories. Stories especially for her, while I revelled in my new status with my small daughter. That went on, until the night she told me, with what could have been regret in her voice, that she " . . . could read her own 'tories out of her very own book . . ." But she didn't say "'tories" And I think I was sorry.

I never wrote down any of those "'tories." They were for the ears of my little girl only. Somehow I couldn't bring myself to put them on paper. For they had a special meaning; they were a special bond between us -- a something that bridged the chasm that was subtly forming between us -- a something I didn't want to share with anyone but her. I never have. I never will.

But, from making up those tales for her, I must have been learning how to tell other stories that would hold the attention and interest of young minds. I must have been learning the basic concept of story-telling for kids -- how to appeal to the intellect and the heart of kids, and to keep abreast of that intellect, and that heart -- and change with them as they changed.

It was a long time before I got around to doing any writing for kids. After all, the market wasn't, and still isn't, a very profitable one. The word length is still tight, the editors exacting, the requirements narrow, and the pay -- well, shall we say it isn't all that generous, except for one magazine that pays up to twenty-five cents per word, an amazing sum for any publication. But it is a cheerful, happy, challenging field; one in which the writer will learn about human nature -- small fry type and otherwise.

A nationally known children's writer once raised eyebrows at a seminar when he said that kids liked to read "dirty books." He hastened to explain that he didn't mean pornography, kid style, but books on library shelves that were *dirty* because of being handled by so many grimy hands. When I checked with a librarian, she laughed. "He's right," she said. "Children want to read books that other children read, or have read. So they look on the shelves for books that are somewhat worse for wear. The dirtier a book is, the more kids have read it, and the more other kids want to read it. The highest compliment the children can pay a writer is to get his books dirtier than any others on the shelves."

Out of the mouths -- and grubby hands -- of babes . . .

When I got around to trying to write for the kids' magazines, I did fairly well -- at first. Then I started to get nice notes from the editors, but my scripts came back with them. After a few such brush-offs, I did some realistic appraising.

It didn't take long to spot the trouble. When I compared my rejects with what the juveniles were publishing, I found that I was merely writing adult stories, with adult plots, adult situations, and using juvenile characters. The dialogue wasn't kid's dialogue; the thinking and action weren't the thinking and action of kids. And I was having adults step in and solve the problems the kids were struggling with, instead of letting the kids do their own resolving.

After a few more near-misses, I suddenly hit upon the idea of pretending it was twenty years before; that I had just come home from a road trip; that I was sitting on the side of a little girl's bed, telling a "'tory" to a tiny tyke with big eyes. I was once more telling a kid's story to a kid. My little girl. It worked. And it still works.

Now, when I write a kid story, it's strictly formula, but the formula is the one my small daughter taught me so long ago. My locales aren't the frozen wastes of Alaska, or Labrador, or the North Pole. Rather, most of my kid stories have a railroad background, and are laid in the days before the coming of the "white-faces," the diesel-electric locomotives that replaced the monstrous smoke-and-fire-breathing steam locomotives, the huge black hulks of brass-trimmed iron and steel that have faded into history, taking with them so much of the romance that was railroading when we old-timers were young.

My characters are always kids. While grown-ups seem to have lost interest in railroads since the coming of the diesel-electrics, the kids sure haven't forgotten. So my characters, boys and girls alike, still find a thrill in the thunder of the exhaust, the smell of coal smoke and hot oil, the hissing of pent-up steam, the eerie whine of a headlight generator, the indescribable sound of releasing air brakes, the clank of metal on metal, the haunting deep-throated chime of a steam whistle, unlike any sound anywhere else, the rhythmic clang-clang of brass bells. Kids still hold the steam locomotives in awe -- along with the big, burly, kindly railroad men, themselves a link with a tradition of the past . . .

My readers are always a part of the action. Through them my readers see and hear the locomotives, the trains, and know the men who make them go. There is always some problem, some catastrophe, some crisis. The lead character is always the hero -- or the heroine -- one with whom the youthful reader can identify, in whom the reader can believe.

At a recent Writers' Conference, someone asked me what essentials there had to be in a kids' story. Best I can remember, my reply went something like this:

"First, kids want the *characters they read about to be kids*, not watered down grown-ups. The lead character must be in the first scene, and the spotlight must be focused on that character all through the story.

"Second, there must always be a *problem;* one involving the lead character. The problem must be solved, or resolved, practically always by the lead. It's okay to have a grown-up help solve the problem, but the grown-up must be motivated by the kids in the story.

"One mistake too many of us make is to begin a story with adults talking about their offspring. Nothing turns a kid off more quickly than that device. *Start with the kid* -- age, background, characteristics; enough detail to enable the young reader to create a word picture. Let the story grow and develop through the eyes, the ears, the voice of the kid. And let it end happily. Always happily, with the reader feeling as rewarded and as satified as the subject of the story is.

"The *dialogue* must be in keeping with the characters. *Kids must talk like kids.* I don't say that you should stick to 'approved word-lists,' but I do say that college level conversation among first-graders leaves me cold, yet I see it almost every time I read a kids' magazine.

"As to *plot structure*, it doesn't have to always be first-reader simple. Today's kids aren't all that unsophisticated. I prefer the straight-line plot, with few deviations. I don't mind giving away a few of the standard plots I've used, most of which were based on real-life incidents.

"Years ago, my daughter brought two baby blue-jays into the house, assuring us that they 'felled from the nest.' Well, maybe, but my daughter was quite a tree-climber. The parent blue-jays found their offspring and raised such a racket that we put them out in the yard, from where the irate mother bird wing-whipped her wandering children all the way into the woods, schreeching like a banshee. I turned that one into a story, managing to get a little nature-lore into it, to assure my daughter that 'wild creatures know how to take care of their children without any help from people.'

"Years later, my daughter's dog cornered a duck that had wandered away from a public park. I turned the mutt into a Laborador retriever, the duck into a Canada goose which had been shot down, let the little girl heroine nurse the goose back to health, then had her mate come back for her when the wild geese flew back North in the Spring. My point there was that wild geese mate for life, and remember each other.

"Another time my daughter's dog killed a mother opossum, and my daughter rescued several baby opposums from the animal's pouch. When they grew up, we took them out in the woods and released them. They were immediately at home. That made another nature story, emphasizing the resourcefulness of wild creatures, even if they had been reared among people.

"When we moved to our present home, there was a Greek family next door. The older boy had evidently been given a hard time because of his ancestry, even telling me " . . . I've got a secret, Mr. McLarn. I'm Greek . . ." His grandfather, who lived with them, didn't speak any English, so I bought a Greek phrase book and learned enough Greek to speak with him. That became a story, in which a little boy tried to make friends with the Greek boy next door, failed, bought a phrase book, learned some Greek -- enough to understand the grandfather when he had a heart attack to know what to do. That story was published, and put on cassettes for distribution to subscribers. My point there was that differences in ethnic backgrounds weren't as important as people.

"The essentials? There aren't many. Continuity of character, realistic dialogue, believable problems, consistent solutions, little overt adult participation, and a rewarding, warm, happy ending."

I consider myself doubly fortunate. Not only in having a background of a lifetime of railroading to draw upon for incidents, atmosphere, personalities -- more than I can possibly use -- but also because I have two of the best made-to-order "heros" and one "heroine" for my tales that any writer could dare hope for, in the persons of my two now teen-age grandsons and my one granddaughter. Whenever I need a kid character, I let my mind take me back to the point in time in one of those three lives when one of them was the age of the lead in my tale.

There is one small problem, however. The older boy, now a college freshman, has been featured in several of my works, including one re-printed in a Basal Reader used in schools the kids attended. As he was readily identifiable -- I used his name -- he became an "instant celebrity." To mollify the other lad, I hastily came up with another story, with him, by name, the lead character. When that one was published, my popularity with my granddaughter took a nose-dive. So I wrote another story featured in the Christmas issue of a top-flight juvenile magazine, using all three of the kids -- by name, of course -- but with my granddaughter as the "motivator," and with the illustrations showing her (the excellent artist at the slick-paper magazine copied her pixie features from a photograph I sent him) and with the boys relegated to secondary roles. But they forgave me -- eventually.

No, I don't make much money out of these little 1,500-word tales. The editors are pretty adamant about word-lengths; most of them preferring very short stories, but a few do go that high. Review the juvenile section of WRITER'S MARKET before you send somebody the wrong length, and get it back by return mail.

Because of the short lengths and the low word-rate, I've never been able to explain to the local writing fraternity what keeps me writing for kid books. At my last seminar, a lady asked me why I didn't " . . . do more serious writing, instead of fooling around with kid stuff . . ."

I don't try to explain it any more. I just know that I am content to remember the look in my little girl's eyes in those long-ago years. I am content to remember her saying, "Daddy, you tell the *goodest* 'tories!" And not long ago, my oldest grandson confided that he "wanted to be a writer . . ."

So what if the checks I get aren't eye-popping? What if I do get an occasional "sorry, but . . ." from one of my editors? I can use the money in any shape, form or quantity. But I'm not writing kid stories for money. I'm writing them for the kids. And I'm being paid for them in coin no mint could ever produce.

8 Article Writing—Bait, Hook, Line, and Sinker

Interviewer: *Mr. McLarn, this may be a foolish question, but why do you spend so much time writing those short articles when you could make more money writing full-length material? Aren't you wasting —?*

Me: *Young lady, there's no such thing as a foolish question. But there are plenty of foolish answers. And I hope I'm not giving you one when I tell you that no time spent in writing anything is ever wasted. And despite what you may have heard, if you get into the right field, you can do pretty well financially.*

Generally, article writing *is* hard work (for *me* it is, anyway) and not all that much fun, except in the "personal experience" area. You can enjoy yourself there. I sure did.

Yes, writing modern day articles is pretty hard work. Magazines are drying up, editors are getting pretty choosy, and the competition is keen. I know one writer who is rapidly nearing her thousandth article, and she says things are tough all over.

In spite of what some of the business books say, however, article-writing pays pretty well. If a writer has a flair for research, a certain smooth glibness of style, and enjoys sticking to facts (which I do not) they can make some nice money, as well as a name for themselves.

A big-time article writer once told me:

"Writing a good article is comparable to going fishing. You have to have the right bait; a hook sharp enough and rugged enough to snag the fish you are after; a line strong enough to hold the critter until you get him into the boat -- and not have such a heavy sinker on your line as to drag your whole rig down into the bottom mud and weeds."

I'm no great shakes as a fisherman, but he had something there.

First comes the "bait." The title. As the bait has to be attractive enough and alluring enough to get the attention of the "fish," so must the title of an article have enough eye-catching appeal to make the reader who might be idly leafing through the pages of a magazine stop and look again at a title that fairly jumps out at him.

I've said before that I didn't spend too much time on writing titles, knowing that the editor would change my title on a piece anyhow. They just about always do -- on fiction. But I can't recall many instances of an editor appreciably changing my title on an article. I suppose this is because I tried to hit upon a combination of words for a title that would make *me* stop and look again, and still not reveal too much of what the piece was about. If it caught *my* eyes, even if I did write it, I could be fairly certain that it would do the same for a prospective reader.

Back in the Roosevelt days (Franklin, not Teddy -- I don't date back *that* far!), I was intrigued with that deep resonant voice of his, and that "*Mah Friends*" he used so effectively. Many years later, I began to use "My Friends" in article titles. "My Friends, the Doctors," "My Friends, the Salesmen," "My Friend, my Ulcer" were a few of them. I used that style of title so many times that the editors began to address their letters to me as "Mah Friend Jack." One of them scribbled on the bottom of an acceptance letter, "This 'Mah Friend' isn't particularly original, but it seems to work. My nitpicking copy readers haven't blue-pencilled it yet, but if you come up with a 'My Friends, the Editors,' *I* will!

The title is the bait. See that it's fresh, interesting, and suited to the "fish" you're trying to catch.

My fisherman friend's second point, about the "hook," obviously related to the beloved "narrative hook" we hear so much about in the creative writing courses. The narrative hook, so we are told, is the device that pulls the reader into the piece -- hooks him. Well, maybe. But the "bait," the title, should have already taken care of that little chore. The first sentence, the "lead" is where the hook takes hold and digs in. If the fisherman's hook is the wrong size -- too small or too big -- the smart fish is going to tear loose, wriggle free, or maybe not even get the thing into his mouth. But if it's the right size, neither too big nor too small nor too flimsy, it will set in the piscatorial jaw, and stay there. So it is with the article "lead." Make it too puny, too vague, and it won't hold the reader. Too weighty, too ponderous, too stuffy, and the reader will pass it up, and look for something that doesn't put such a strain on his mentality.

I once wrote a tongue-in-cheek article about some of my neighbors. My lead was this:

> "*The people next door are cat people. Not that they sit on the back fence and yowl all night. But they own -- or are owned by -- a couple of slant-eyed demoniac prize-winning Siamese felines. Chang and Yang are their names. And what they do to Louie-V, my stupid Boxer, shouldn't happen to a dog . . .*"

When the piece was published in a Canadian weekly news magazine, it brought me a dozen letters, including one from a university creative writing teacher, who told me that she used that lead in her classroom work, because, ". . . it made your reader yours forevermore, right from the start!"

Another lead, to an article on "Supervision," brought a few letters, too:

> *"With my education, my background and my experience, what can I possibly bring to these people, who know me not from Adam, and care less? What can they possibly learn from me?"*

Some of the letters were complimentary, but one unsigned scrawl singed my ears with, "*You don't need to wonder, friend. You didn't promise anything, so you didn't have to deliver. But you at least made me mad enough to read your damned article, and I guess that's what the lead was intended to do . . .*"

The objective in article-writing is to immediately grab the reader's attention with the title, and keep that attention with the lead. But fish have been known to take the hook, come to the surface, and spit the thing right back into the fisherman's eye, such as my anonymous friend did. They have also been known to break the line. So even if you've hooked your "fish," your readers, unless you have a strong enough line to hold you'll surely lose them to the cross-word puzzle or the comics.

This brings up the little item of "consistency." Nothing is more annoying to a reader than to settle back to read an article with an intriguing title and a beguiling lead, and then along about the fourth paragraph have the whole thing fizzle out into padding and pablum.

I know of no way to guard against this, other than to do something I literally abhor -- make a pre-writing outline of the piece; put down on paper every point, every illustration you expect to use, read it over, and see if you "feel" each of them with the same general intensity, or close to it.

Chances are that if you could graph your reactions the way an EKG unit monitors your heart action, your graphic print-out would have roller-coaster-like peaks and valleys all over the chart. To build the readers expectations up to fever pitch in a few well-done paragraphs, only to drop them into a mass of dull, pedantic blaaaah is equivalent to using a flimsy line to haul in an annoyed bass. Your line has to be strong enough to hold any fish you expect to snag, all the way up to the spindle of your Shakespeare -- and your article has to be strong enough to hold your reader with the same even, unrelaxed tension, all the way to "The End."

Sometimes we characters who do our fishing with worms make the mistake of putting too heavy a sinker on our line. That drags our baited hook too deep in the water, pulls our bobber down too far, and makes for a dreary session, fish-wise. Get too "weighty" in your article -- subject matter, wordage, style -- and your piece sinks to the bottom and stays there.

But article-writing needn't always be heavy going; not even if you're writing about Aztec pottery or Nuclear fission. Unless you have an assignment to write something "to order" that sends you slogging up to here through volumes of history or medicine or science or whatever, don't be so all-fired stuffy! You're supposed to get some fun out of writing, remember? So, if you can avoid them, stay clear of the ponderous subjects; skim through a few magazines you like to read, and try to top something they have.

Article writing *can* be fun. In no other area can the writer express himself so honestly and so completely. In no other field will the "real you" come through so readily, so satisfyingly -- if you will but let it. And there is something about seeing your words in printed typeface that brings an elation nothing else does -- even if you find yourself wondering why the hell you said such a stupid thing!

I learned this long ago, from my first "personal experience" article.

I had just suffered through a particularly harrowing medical episode -- one that came pretty close to taking me away from here. Until then, I had never given a thought to writing "fact articles" of any kind. Out of the hospital, weak, restless, bored, trying to get up enough strength to go back to my job, I scribbled off an article, mainly to rib my Agent, who had a thing about hospitals and sick people.

I sent the piece to him as a gag. He took me to task for writing about such a grisly subject, and the next thing I knew he had sold the piece, to a "Health" magazine!

I hadn't used my own name on the article, for fear that my doctor might not take kindly to some of the more caustic comments I made about the whole medical profession. He did find out that I wrote it, and the guy used the article in a paper he presented at a medical convention, to illustrate the thinking of an ungrateful cuss whom he had literally dragged back from wherever it is that patients in my condition and with my past life were supposed to go. It has shown up in various forms in various magazines and newspapers for many years. Sometimes I get a few bucks for "reprint rights," but mostly I don't. I really don't mind, for MY FRIEND, MY ULCER opened up a whole new field of writing to me.

After MY FRIEND, MY ULCER, I didn't do much in the way of article writing. But the feeling persisted that there might be a kind of therapy in article writing; that it offered a retreat from reality, an outlet for feelings that would otherwise be bubbling and boiling inside me, thereby making me a prime prospect for a re-run of what happened to me in the first place and prompted the article.

I suppose the idea really jelled when I had another episode, this one even tougher than the first, winding up with me in surgery, involved with one of the grisliest operations in the book, followed by a sojourn in the hospital that still gives me nightmares when I remember it.

When I finally could face a typewriter again, I really let myself go. I turned out an article that, in addition to letting me get a few gripes off my chest, caused a three-cornered shouting match with an irate hospital administrator and a particularly obnoxious nursing supervisor, and brought me a letter from one of my former hospital ward-mates of the MY FRIEND, MY ULCER days, congratulating me for, " . . . finally having the guts to speak your mind, instead of keeping on being that damned cheerful 'nice guy' you were while we were sharing the room I'm still trying to die in!"

From the flood of letters, vituperative and otherwise; from the calls and visits resulting from MY FRIENDS, MY DOCTORS, it seems that some of my fellow sufferers got something out of what I wrote, and maybe a little comfort, too. One letter I shall always treasure read:

> *"If a guy like you can come through what you did and still be able to laugh about it, maybe I won't be so scared when I go up for the same surgery next week. Thanks, friend, for helping me to stop worrying and start concentrating on making it . . ."*

The letter was unsigned, so I never knew who sent it, or how he came out "next week." I prayed that he'd make it.

As a footnote to what I said about writing time never being "wasted," I recently had my theory confirmed. I wrote a short piece on salesmanship for a sales magazine. A month later a big-time book publisher in the business field wrote me in care of the magazine, asking me if I would consider writing a book for him on "Sales Psychology."

Flattered no end, but a little embarrassed, I wrote back that I didn't want to mislead him, that I was not really a salesman, but a business writer. Back came a reply, suggesting that I do two books, one on selling, the other on management. "You haven't disqualified yourself," he quipped. "But you've just broadened your horizons!"

I'm still mulling it over. Two books? Sheesh!

The point is pretty clear. Everything you write puts your name before just that many more people. Just that many more prospective outlets for your material. No, you don't "waste time" by writing the small stuff. You just "broaden your horizons!"

Can you write "personal articles?" Of course you can. Everybody has the capability to do it. All you have to do is to learn to let yourself go – say what's on your mind, what's in your heart. By writing "personal articles," you not only help yourself, but you help a lot of other people. You're not the only one whose problems are getting you down. Let somebody else know how you handle yours, and maybe the other person's troubles won't seem all that bad.

Just let yourself go, on paper. You'll be surprised to find out how easy it is.

9 "Herewith for Review" (Book Reviewing)

Interviewer: *Mr. McLarn, while we were talking about business and educational writing, you mentioned book reveiwing. When I was going through your morgue file --*
Me: *My morgue file? How appropriate!*
Interviewer: *Oh, come on! I was just going to say that I ran across the tear sheets of some book reviews you wrote years ago. Don't you still do book reviews, along with your other writing?*
Me: *Not much any more. But I did have a lot of fun while I was doing them. Learned a lot, too . . .*

I think the first book review I ever wrote was of an excellent book by Carl Carmer, back in the 1930's. The title was "Stars Fell on Alabama". There was a popular song by that title, too. As a native of Alabama, the book intrigued me, I bought a copy, found it fascinating, and wrote a one-page review. As far as I know, the review was never published.

I got into active reviewing several years later, for a local newspaper. The book editor was in a hurry for some up-to-date reviews; somebody told him about me and my free-lancing; he sent me three books, and my career as a book reviewer got off the ground.

Reviewing books isn't all that hard -- unless you permit it to be. I made the mistake of doing that. While many reviewers first read the book-jacket blurbs, skim through the book, pick out a few passages, put them into some kind of order, bang out five hundred words or so, and forget the whole deal, I went all out. I ignored the book-jacket splash, and read the whole book – sometimes twice. And I usually wrote the review twice – once to get the feel of what the author was trying to say, and once to figure out what the author was really saying.

My first few reviews were mercilessly blue-penciled by the book editor, who had the uncanny ability to sense when I got too far afield on a book, and didn't hesitate to bring me back onto the reservation. It was from that editor that I learned what book reviewing was all about. It was not only what the reviewer was doing for the book and its author, but also what book reviewing was doing for the reviewer. What it was doing for me.

I've always had a healthy respect for anybody who has the stamina and the patience to write a book. I had plenty of trouble turning out a few thousand acceptable words of short material, and to think that there were people who could sit at a typewriter day after day, writing and re-writing a book of a hundred thousand words or so was downright incredible. So my reviews usually started off with a tribute to the author, and a confession of my own temerity for being so presumptuous as to write, as the book editor put it, " . . . these little essays on other people's work . . ."

The second time I used this kind of lead-in, the editor called me up. "Look, McLarn," he said. "Quit being so damned humble, will you? You're doing these people favors by even reading their stuff, much less analyzing it, and you don't owe anybody any apologies. My kids are always telling me to 'tell it like it is.' Do it!"

That ended my era of the apologetic lead-in. In later years I found other editors singing the same song -- not only in the book review columns but in every other field in which I wrote. "Don't apologize. Just 'tell it like it is." In whatever kind of writing you do . . . "

I have no idea as to how many books I reviewed during the next few years. One wall of the den in my daughter's Harbor View home in Charleston, South Carolina, is lined, floor to ceiling, with books I reviewed. Every time I go to Charleston, I browse through those books, every one of which has become a treasured friend. They are friends, because I made them, and their authors, friends. I did this by, every time I wrote a review, sending a copy to the author, and pasting the newspaper or magazine review tear-sheet on the inside cover of the book. And the authors answered, too! I pasted their letters inside the books, thus making them, to me, at least, collectors items.

Many of those writers are dead now. Others have stopped writing. But still others are continuing to turn out thousands of words of successful prose each year. And once in a while I hear from one of my old "subjects," just wanting to know if I'm still around. And there is no sentiment in writing?

Book reviewing is a delightfully rewarding pastime for a practicing author. Delightful, for the sheer pleasure it can bring. Rewarding for what the reviewer learns about writing from the successful old pros who "do books." But it has its pitfalls and its heartaches, too. I still remember a book that was written near the end of the Japanese conflict. I don't recall the name, but it was written in grisly detail about the treatment of American captives on a Japanese troop ship. It was so horrifying that I got caught up in the tale, and in my review pulled out all the stops.

When the review was published, it was given a featured spot on a Sunday book page. When I read the printed, slightly edited version, I had the uneasy feeling that maybe I had gone beyond the objectivity and restraint expected of a reviewer, and had permitted myself to do some editorializing of my own.

I was not only right, I was prophetic. A week later, in the "Letters to the Editor" column, there was a "reply" to my review, and was it a dilly! The writer was quite an all-stops-puller-outer himself. Among other things, he called me a warmonger, an unchristian so-and-so, a bigot, a right-winger of a rabble-rouser, and accused me of immeasurably setting back the chances of there ever being peace between the brutal Americans and the downtrodden, misunderstood Japanese!

That little hassle set my teeth on edge. One day, I told myself, I would write an article about reviewing, and the first thing I would say would be that the reviewer should not consider himself or herself an authority on anything, but should stick to reporting, avoiding any personal comments, limiting personal bias of whatever nature, and remembering that it is for the reader of the review to form the reader's own opinions. In other words, as my book editor friend had pounded into me, "Tell it like it is -- not like how you want it to be!"

However, being pretty thin-skinned, the bitterness that my critic had spewed all over me still rankled. I wrote a dozen rebuttals to his diatribe, all of which wound up in the round file. I had finally written what I considered a masterpiece of restrained invective, and was about to mail it to my editor, along with the request that he give it "equal time." But before I stamped the envelope, the mail came. In it was a clipping of another "Letter to the Editor."

"I think it's a shame," the writer said. "That Mr. McLarn should be subjected to such a vicious attack for his admittedly tough review of the book about the troop-ship. After all, he didn't write the book; he just reported what was in it, and his review made me want to read it for myself. So what if he did make some positive statements about it? When this country becomes so repressive that a reviewer, a reporter, or anybody else can't make positive statements about something in which he or she believes without being crucified, we've really got something to worry about . . ."

I tore up my vituperative letter, and turned on the record player. Paul Whiteman had never sounded so good.

I can't give much worth-while advice on book reviewing. I know it isn't for everybody. But for those of us who do find the time and have the inclination to do it, perhaps we should remember a few completely unrelated items.

First -- and I can't emphasize this too strongly -- the reviewer should avoid using the books reviewed as forums for personal prejudices, likes, or dislikes. I remember one instance in which a reviewer started out competently reviewing a book on Birds of the Americas, wrote one sparkling paragraph about the book and its author -- and veered off into a tirade about the brutal repression of minorities! How that reviewer managed that is still beyond my comprehension. Sure, it's a great temptation for a reviewer to use a review to air personal idiosyncrasies, but the readers of your review couldn't care less about your personal politics, your sex, your religion, or what you think about the Panama Canal; they merely want to know in a general way what's in the book, so they can judge whether or not to spend $14.95 for it.

Second, the reviewer should remember that the review will be read, not only by people who buy and read books, but by booksellers who have to decide which of the scads of hard and soft covers that will be plugged by book salesmen. One such bookseller told me, "I value your kind of reviews, Mr. McLarn, because somewhere in them I can usually find a hint of how you think the book is going to sell. Sometimes you goof, but mostly you give us a pretty good idea of a book's potential."

Third, remember the libraries. Most of them operate on a pretty skimpy budget, and have to depend upon reviewers to judge whether or not to stock a particular volume. The "dirty book" syndrome applies here, too -- if a book bears the look of being handled, it's a pretty safe bet that some reviewer did a good job of selling the book to the librarian responsible for guessing right most of the time.

Finally, in addition to the service the reviewer performs for the reading public, there's the service the reviewer performs for himself or herself. I mentioned before that I regarded the books I reviewed, and the authors who wrote them, as old friends. As I remember the books in my daughter's den, where, hopefully, some day her kids will delve into the ones I reviewed, read the reviews, and the letters from authors that still leave me misty-eyed, and reflect upon "writing as it used to be," I like to think that maybe, because of me and my reviewing, they'll have a better insight into writing as it was a generation or so ago.

Just the other day, I ran across a book I reviewed by one of the better known writers of a few years ago. The book had a trick ending; one which sent me, slightly red-faced, back over it, to see where and how the author had so cleverly sent me down blind alleys. When I sent him a copy of the review, in his reply he said:

"I'm so glad you enjoyed the book; particularly that you didn't see through the deception until the end. I tried to be scrupulously fair over this. Of course, the book is really an exercise designed to show how we bring our ingrained prejudices to bear down on what we are reading . . ."

Do I treasure that letter? You bet I do!

I still remember a letter from that same author, about another book of his I reviewed:

"Thank you very much indeed for sending me a copy of your review. This was a most generous appreciation, and, as before, you seem to have divined exactly what I was aiming at, which in this case was personal and total honesty -- the mistakes and failures accorded just as much prominence as the things which went right. It gives plenty of ammunition to the enemy, but who cares about that? The battle is on my own ground. . ."

My book editor hasn't sent me any more of this author's books for a long time. I wish the lady would -- especially since this particular author wrote me that he "hoped he would one day be able to review one of my own books . . ."

There are many more such letters down in Charleston. But one I particularly treasure came from an author who is no longer living. He wrote many books, and I reviewed several of them, but two I remember were outstanding, one being about his boyhood with his grandfather, and the other about his life as a young man. They were so heart-warmingly delightful that I gave my review copies to my two grandsons. When I sent the author copies of my reviews -- which were laudatory -- he came back with, "Mister, you are exactly right. I didn't write those two books for money. I wrote them because I had to -- and you knew it . . ."

Is book reviewing rewarding? Definitely. At least for me. But book reviewers, like old soldiers, sometimes just "fade away." They just get tired. And book editors get promoted, retire, resign, get fired, whatever. Their replacements have their own stable of writers who do reviews. Once in a while I do get a book -- something about railroading, maybe, or history, or politics -- but not very often. And yes, I do miss them. But I guess it's just as well. Viewpoints change, writing changes, reviewers change. Besides, I do have to mow the lawn once in a while.

Do I advise you to get into reviewing? Not really. But if you do, you will get far more out of the reading and study and writing and rewriting you will have to do than the author or the book editor will. Your subconscious mind will store up in its "memory bank" the kind of information you will need if and when you decide to "do" a book on your own. Too, you'll acquire a whole new, positive outlook on the entire field of literary endeavor. And if you ever do get your book published, well, you'll have printer's ink in your veins, forevermore.

How do you get into reviewing? Simple enough. Pick up the telephone, call the book editor at your local newspaper, and say, "Look, I'm a free-lance writer. I'd like to do book reviews for you. How about putting me on your list for --" and tell the editor something about yourself, and the kind of books you'd like to review. You might get a fast brush-off; some newspapers prefer to use their staff writers as reviewers. But you might get an assignment. And when your review comes out, it will probably be edited drastically, to make it conform to space requirements. But your name will be on it; you'll immediately become known to your local writing fraternity; you'll probably be invited to attend some club meetings. If so, go. But most of all, remember that you're having fun! If it isn't fun, don't do it.

> **Interviewer:** *Okay. My second question is, how much do you get per review -- usually?*
> **Me:** *As I said before, the only fee I ever got for a review was the priviledge of keeping the book. Hopefully, you'll do better. I never did, but it was fun.*

10 "Me Write a Book? You've Got to be Kidding!"

Interviewer: *Mr. McLarn, have you ever thought of doing a book?*
Me: *"Doing a book?" Doesn't anybody ever "write" books any more?*
Interviewer: *Oh, come on! If you were to "do" -- sorry -- to "write" a book, how would you start?*
Me: *By having my head examined for holes. Me write a book? You've got to be kidding!*

I wasn't exactly honest with the young lady that morning. Sure, I had thought about writing -- or "doing" -- a book. Every writer has visions of seeing his name on a hard-cover, on a book-club contract worth upwards of twenty thousand dollars, on a half million paper-backs cluttering up newsstands. Every writer who has sold even a single penny-a-word article to some obscure publication dreams of being jetted first-class to New York, to sign contracts, attend publishers' cocktail parties, getting writer's cramp autographing his best-sellers, having Hollywood agents call in the middle of the night begging for the screen rights to his latest thriller. Of course they do! And I'm certainly no exception.

But up until recently I suppose I did differ in some respects from most of my fellow literary dreamers. Whenever I thought about "that book," my inherently lazy alter ego made itself felt. It reminded me how big money writers freely admit to taking as many as five years, even ten, to do the research, the brain-busting, the writing and other chores involved in a book. It pointed out that being cooped up with a typewriter while the fish were jumping in the harbor, or the grandchildren wanted to take me sailing was downright silly. And there was the tedium of writing, re-writing and writing again, which any book requires, along with those yard-long galley proofs to be read and corrected, with every change made coming out of my royalties and my hide.

Adding to that the squirming over "reviews," those caustic little essays tinged with blood and written in vitriol by critics whose "lightest word would harrow up my soul, freeze my aging blood, and stand each hair upon my head . . . like the quills of a fretful porcupine . . ." made me doubt that such a thin-skinned soul as mine would survive such a traumatic experience.

Finally, the thought of the thousands of books better than I could ever write that are printed every year -- most of which are lucky to sell as many as nine hundred and twenty-seven copies, along with the wonder if there would be room in my bedroom closet for that stack of "publisher's remainders" that would be shipped to me -- collect -- when the unsold copies of the book over which I labored for so long would have to be cleared from the publisher's warehouse, to make room for some other poor guy's literary fiasco, ballooned my fear into abject, cowardly terror.

Sure, I had thought about "doing a book." But up until then only negatively. That silent voice within me, the voice of the hard-nosed business man I really am, had been saying, loud and clear, "Look, stupid, stick to your short stories and your articles, mow the lawn and edge the walk. These things you know something about. Book? You? Naaaah!"

I had all but dismissed the whole idea from my mind as

being fraught with too many negatives, too many problems, when all the negatives and most of the problems were solved in one telephone call. Yes, I've "done a book." A full-length, 100,000 word, third-person novel. As a "ghost."

Not long before the charming interviewer and her recording machine showed up on my patio there came the strangest telephone call of my career. It was from the president of one of the corporations making up a huge conglomerate in another state. His boss, the Chairman of the Board of the conglomerate had an idea that the story of his own adult life would make quite a book. He didn't have the time to do it himself, and was looking for somebody to take the material he would provide and put it into the form of a novel. He had seen my name in some business publications, and if I would be interested in taking on the job, he'd like for me to come and talk about it.

I was so startled that I couldn't even answer him. The gentleman must have taken my silence as an indication of reluctance, for he went on to say that I could practically name my own price for the job.

Still feeling like a character in a dream, I made an appointment with the would-be author, in his plush office suite. Both he and the president who worked for him were astonishingly young, and, to my surprise, were willing to listen to what I had to say about writing -- including my admission that I had never undertaken anything so ambitious as "doing a book."

To my further surprise, they didn't think my lack of experience in novel writing would disqualify me. Instead, they considered it an asset, because I wouldn't be "bound by a lot of hackneyed rules and 'taboos'."

"I just want you to write the story as though I were writing it, McLarn," said the Chairman. "I want you to think as I do, talk as I do, act and react as I do. You fellows can work out the financial details. How do you want the material furnished? Do you just talk to me, or what?"

A couple of hours later we had indeed worked out the details. He would talk -- not dictate -- the story he wanted to tell into a cassette recorder. I would transcribe the material, edit it, rearrange it, put it into novel form, and keep on working with it until I came up with a satisfactory script. As to money, we agreed upon a flat fee, paid half upon delivery of the script, the other half on publication. After publication, I would receive a percentage of the net proceeds of the book, and if the movies picked it up, a share of the profits would come to me.

Who could turn down an offer like that? Especially when the "flat fee" they offered was an eye-popping one to the likes of me!

When the cassettes started showing up in my mail, I began a whole new experience in writing. I wasn't unused to tape recorders; I had used dictating machines for years, but had always been on the input end. Two months and 100,000 words later I had developed sore fingers, and a healthy respect for the people who had transcribed my business dictations for so many years.

I soon realized that my client knew what he was doing. He knew the story he was going to tell. And, as with most first novels, it was semi-biographical. His narration hung together well, his dictation was flawless. There was only one problem -- he talked in the first person, but wanted his book in the third person. I tried converting from first to third person as I transcribed, but it was too slow; I found myself more interested in the words than in the story. So I did the only thing I could do -- transcribed the first-person narration exactly as it flowed from the recorder, then converted it into third person.

When I finished those two tasks, totaling some 200,000 words of typing, the real work began. First, I had to break the story down into chapters. That wasn't too big a job. I had one of those bellows-type partitioned envelopes used for sorting papers. The story seemed to automatically divide itself into chapters, so I paper-clipped the related pages together and dropped them into the appropriate sections of the sorter.

I had read somewhere that the modern novel chapter ran

about 2,500 words -- ten typewritten pages. My narrator couldn't say "hello" in 2,500 words, even with my somewhat ruthless editing. So I settled upon 5,000 word chapters -- the same word-length I had used in short-story work for so many years. I calculated that I could turn out 5,000 words, twenty pages, every two days, so in about forty working days the job would be completed, and I would have a novel.

It didn't work out that way. When I went over the draft of the book, I got a shock. The story line was excellent. The dialogue was good. But the lead character -- my thinly disguised narrator – came through as a cold, colorless, humorless, unemotional individual who set my teeth on edge. And I knew, from my meetings with him, and from the voice on the tapes, he wasn't that way at all.

After wrestling with the problem for a while, it suddenly occured to me to talk to the man's wife. I called her, explained my difficulty, and asked if I could come and talk to her. She laughed. "I hoped you would come to see me," she said. "I think I can tell you about the man my husband really is, instead of what he tries to make people think he is. He's really a love!"

I did go to see her, with my own tape recorder. An hour later I had the real story of the man, in the words of the woman who loved him. I still have that tape. It's beautiful.

Once more I wrote the story -- another hundred thousand words, in which I made liberal use of the quirks of character, the intimate behavior, the by-play with his children -- everything that made him a real person instead of a wooden, stock character. He literally came to life. When I completed the third draft, I took it to the man who had commissioned me.

"This isn't the final draft of the book," I said. "It's a rough draft. I want your boss to read it, and tell me if we're in the same ball-park."

It was several weeks before I heard any more from the project. Then I was summoned to the office of the conglomerate. My manuscript was returned to me, bearing enough corrections, additions and deletions to require a one hundred percent re-write. I learned later that the manuscript had been passed around to several of the people who, although somewhat dis-guised, were readily identifiable in the story. Some of them liked my interpretation of their characters and their personal-ities. Some didn't -- in spades.

But by then I had gotten into the swing of things. I made the corrections, the deletions, the additions, all right. But this time I didn't stick to the script. Instead I holed up in a beach cottage with my tape recorder and typewriter, and replayed the tapes I had so laboriously transcribed. There was a difference. I wasn't listening to the narrator's words. I was listening to the man himself. He had suddenly become human. Little nuances I had completely missed in the previous writing became ob-vious. The narrator's motivations became clear and understand-able. And as I listened, I found myself employing the oldest trick of the writing profession. I literally became the character the book was about.

From there on it was all down hill. I set up a working schedule of ten finished pages per day, every working day. But they were ten final-draft pages, each representing four pages of writing. For every page of finished draft, I finally wrote four, often five, pages. Each day, upon reaching the self-established "goal" of ten pages, I quit, even if in the middle of sentence, read over those ten pages, correcting any mistakes in typing, spelling, syntax, whatever.

How many times that ten-page-goal-and-review resulted in my rewriting a passage, a page, two pages -- ten pages -- I can't remember. I guess what I was doing could be called "polishing the door-knobs," but I took a sort of professional pride in knowing that when I laid those ten pages atop the growing stack of finished product they were error-free -- and, more impor-tantly, that they said exactly what I wanted them to say.

As the novel progressed, I found myself more and more sub-mersed into the character whose life I was portraying, into the personality and the life-style of the man whose voice came so authoritatively, so impressively from the whirring recorder. My thinking and his thinking merged, until I found myself reacting to the forces that surrounded him, the problems with which he struggled, and which all but destroyed him, physically and mentally and spiritually, just as he reacted. So much so that his story became my story. So much so that, when I read the final draft for the last time, all four hundred pages of it, I couldn't begin to tell where the tapes left off and where I began.

The project took, appropriately enough, almost nine months to the day, from inception to delivery of two copies of the completed manuscript. It was with a feeling of both relief and regret that I turned the neatly boxed manuscript over to the author. You don't "live with" a story for nine long months without developing a parental attachment for it, and for the characters who live in it. Oh, sure, I'll get paid for my work, for my nine months "gestation period." But I believe that I gained more from writing those four hundred thousand words -- first draft, second draft, working draft and final -- than mere money.

For instance, I learned that my misgivings about writing a book were not well founded; that a hundred thousand word novel isn't all that big a deal. Until I tackled that job, the longest story I had ever written ran about 6,500 words, and my tales usually ran out of gas at about 5,000 words. It took the novel-writing project to show me that a hundred thousand word novel is really nothing more than twenty 5,000 word tales with the same characters, the same plot, and the same pre-planned ending.

In fact, a novel is a sight easier to put together than an equal number of short pieces, word-wise. Concocting twenty stories means dreaming up twenty reasonably uncribbed-from-somebody-else plots, twenty sets of assorted characters, twenty or more situations, complications, sub-plots, endings, contrived or uncontrived -- whatever. A novel has but one of each of these attributes, even if it is spread over four hundred typewritten pages of the peaks and valleys of the tale.

On the other hand, there are some rules applicable to writing novels that do not restrict the short story writer. For instance, when I start a short story or an article, I rarely have the faintest idea as to what the ending is going to be -- who gets the girl, who marries what guy, how the murder was committed. Half the fun of short story writing -- for the writer -- is to let himself be but a spectator, sitting on an Olympus, watching with tolerant amusement the antics of the puppets that dangle from the strings he holds. I always get a bang out of a minor character I had thrown in for a brief scene suddenly developing into a "take charge" person, and changing the whole trend of the story, perhaps even bringing it to a climax I hadn't even dreamed about.

That's one of the reasons I give for not writing outlines -- it destroys the spontaneity of the story. (The real reason is that I just plain hate to write outlines!)

But that premise just doesn't work that way in a novel. The first question I asked my client on the novel assignment was, "Do you know what your ending is going to be? If you don't, we'd better figure one out now." He did have the ending in mind -- fortunately. Because, even with my lack of novel-writing experience, I had read enough of them to sense that if the author didn't know where he was going before he started, and what road he was going to take, how would he know when he got there? So, in spite of my aversions to outlines and pre-planned endings, I had a pretty fair outline in my head as to what the novel was going to be before I wrote a single paragraph.

The novel writers cannot afford to relax and let their characters do their work for them, as the short story writers can, and most of the time do. In a novel, every character must be kept under rigid discipline; allowed to play the part for which he or she is in the book, and no more. I did let one character get away from me in the book, and start being a little too bitchy, a little too aggressive -- and a whole lot too appealing.

I had to re-do fifty pages to get the woman back on the reservation! After that I made very sure that my people were doing what they were supposed to do -- contribute to the over-all story, and not cater to their own personal gratifications (and mine) as much as I would have liked to. But I couldn't allow myself to forget that I was working for the lead character. He was paying me, so . . .

I don't know when (or if) the novel will ever be published, or "brought out." Business problems being what they are today, conglomerate Board Chairmen are pretty busy people, and maybe my client is too preoccupied with more weighty problems than he had when he first conceived the idea of "doing a book" on himself. My last letter from him mentioned that he was still "scouting around for a publisher." I hope he finds one.

But whether or not the book comes out; whether or not it makes a lot of money; whether or not the book clubs pick it up; whether or not it reaches Hollywood and television, I know what it has already done for me. It uncovered within me a talent I didn't know I had -- an ability to take a stack of recording tapes yea-high, glean from them the life story of a truly big man, and put that story on paper in such a way as to make him entertainingly real.

The only regret I have is that I am a "ghost." That when the book is brought out, it won't have my name on it. I could wish that it would, for there is a lot of me in it. But I can never acknowledge it, and if it makes the big time I can never take any credit for it. Ghosts never do. But I did take one sneaky liberty. As Alfred Hitchcock is known to "sign" his films by playing a cameo part in each of them, so did I "sign" my client's book, by writing myself into one brief scene. I hope it escapes the eagle eyes of the editors and shows up in the printed version.

Will I ever "do" a novel of my own? I really don't know. But I think I do know how -- now. Thanks to two young corporation executives who had enough confidence in me to give me a job I didn't know I could do, and let me do it -- my way.

If I were going to "do" a book of my own, how would I start? By getting off myself, away from a typewriter, away from a telephone, away from everything in any way connected with my present nice, comfortable, routine-less way of life, and take a good, long look at myself; think about everything I have ever done, good and bad; about everything I ever wanted to do and didn't -- everything I didn't want to do, and did.

Then I would decide whether there is anything in my life, good or bad, that would make interesting reading for somebody who knew me not from Adam's off ox. And decide whether I had something worthwhile to say, or the ability to say it if I did.

If, after all that soul-searching, I could convince myself that I did have something to say that people would be able to read without acquiring an acute belly-ache, I'd go back home, back to my typewriter, and write a four-page, thousand word "essay" on that excursion into self-analysis. I would put it away and not even look at or think about it for a week, after which I would "accidentally" run into it. If, upon reading it over one time, I heard a voice say, "Well, stupid, you just might have come up with something. Go ahead, if you want to, but don't say I didn't warn you!" Then, and only then, would I seriously entertain the idea of "doing a book."

Having gone that far, I would be completely, irrevocably hooked. There could be no turning back.

I would thereupon hie myself to the nearest public library and make a list of every book on the shelves of any subject even remotely resembling what I had in mind. I would read every one of those books, even if it took me all my spare time for a month, until I had become so steeped in the knowledge of my gradually jelling subject that other people had so painfully and patiently compiled that I would be like a computer bank, filled with detail ready to be retreived when the right buttons were pushed.

Not that I would think of using all that unrelated, uncoordinated data. No, I would merely be conditioning my own mind, so that my own mental processes would do their thing when the right time came -- so that I would all but hypnotize myself into the same frame of mind as those others before me were in, and who probably did the same thing when they did their own books.

That chore completed, I would write myself a ten or twelve paragraph letter, just as though I were writing to an old friend, telling him what I was up to. Those paragraphs would be pieces of the action eventually, and would automatically convert themselves into chapters when the time came.

I would take that bellows-like sorter I had left over from my ghost writing project, cut the carbon of that letter into paragraphs, and put each paragraph into a pocket. But I wouldn't start writing -- not even an outline, certainly not a first draft. Instead, I'd go about my usual disorganized way of life, with one difference. Each time something occured to me about "the book," I'd scribble it on a card, and drop the card into the proper bellows pocket -- into my crude data bank. I'd keep this up, accumulating more and more random bits of business, until the flashes of inspiration slowed to one or two a day. Then, and only then, would I pull the confused mass of usable and unusable material out of those pockets, put them into some kind of order, and start on my first draft.

Right there is where my business sense might take over. I have never been able to write convincingly about anything I didn't know something about. So at this point the book would begin to take on a personality of its own. My topic, my theme, could no longer be the vague, nebulous idea that it was at the beginning. It would have to take a definite shape and form and purpose.

If I were writing an historical novel, it would be back to the library for me, to read everything specific I could find about the period in which my story would be laid. If it turned out to be a tale of the Old West, I would have to steep myself in the lore of the plains, the Zane Grey type plainsmen, the outlaws, the lawmen, the nesters, the Indians.

If I were to write about a truck driver, I wouldn't need to do much research. I've already done it, during that hair-raising, spine-tingling week-end I spent in the cab of that diesel rig, on twisting mountain roads, in roadside truck stops and diners, everywhere the diesel rigs howl and grind over the highways.

If my book would include court-room scenes, I would haunt the court-house, listening to trials, watching the expressions on the faces of those who run afoul of the law, those who defend it, thwart it, administer it. I would try to wangle a few hours in a patrol car, so that when I wrote about police work I would at least have a passing knowledge of on-the-street law, and the strange language that has grown up around the blue-uniformed symbols of authority -- if not always justice.

And if I needed some exciting sex scenes to embelish my story . . . at your age, McLarn? Forget it!

Right about now my direction would have been established, my course set. I would have researched my subject enough to be at home with it. I would be ready to begin.

My beginning would be simple enough. It would consist of the first four chapters, and the last chapter -- written slowly, thoughtfully, with an eye to continuity and character development -- remembering that I would have to live with the characters for a long time. I would complete those chapters in the best possible manuscript form I was capable of producing. Then, without stopping to admire my own greatness, I would write a taut, concise outline of the remaining chapters, in synopsis form, telling enough about each chapter to make it plain that I had sufficient meat in each to make each worth writing.

I have never used outlines or synopses in writing short stories or articles. Never needed them. But writing a book isn't just writing a short story. It requires discipline and long-range planning, far greater than in any other form of writing.

There would be one seemingly inconsistent factor about the outline. I would outline the last chapter -- but I would also write it completely. There is good reason for this. In short story writing, I would often start out with one premise, one basic idea, and one specific lead character, and suddenly find another premise, another idea, even another lead character taking over the story. I didn't mind -- I rather enjoyed the new twist. So I just let the new development stay, and allowed the new character to run the show, just sticking around myself to see what was going to happen next.

But with a book, the authors must know where they are going, and what they are going to do when they get there. "There" is the final chapter of the book, where all the loose ends come together. Writing the first four chapters and the final chapter boxes the authors in, and if they are any kind of craftspeople at all, they're going to stay within the bounds they impose upon themselves and their characters.

Once I had my first four chapters, my outline, and my final chapter safely written, proof-read, and ready to go somewhere, I would write another letter, this time to a long-time friend, a Literary Agent who has done so well that he doesn't fool with anything but books any more. I would tell him in some detail what I was doing, and ask him if he would be interested in looking at my first-four-chapters-outline-and final chapter package. As for twenty-five years he has known me only as a short-story writer, he'd probably think I had flipped. But he's a nice guy, and I'm reasonably sure he would tell me to send it along, which I would do -- and brace myself for the sky to fall on me.

I fully expect he would find something wrong with everything from the title, the development, the conclusion -- everything but the typing. (He always said he could depend upon me for a good job of typing.) But, old pro that he is, amid his pages of the-bark-on criticism there would be the terse paragraphs of professional brilliance that meant so much to me when I sent him my first offering -- a Confession Story -- twenty-five years ago.

Then would begin the real work. Then would come the rewriting, the rubbing-out-and-starting-over, the ruthless elimination of passages I loved like a child. The re-doing of sentences, paragraphs, pages, even whole chapters; the wiping out of beloved characters, adored scenes; the substitution of other characters, other scenes.

All the while this went on, I would be learning what I had always suspected -- that writing a twenty-chapter book is a hell of a lot more demanding than writing twenty related shorts or articles. That while it isn't too hard to stick to one subject, one set of characters, one theme, for five thousand words, staying within the guide lines, on the same subject, with the same people, the same theme, for a hundred thousand words, is something else again. That while it isn't all that difficult to keep a characterization or a theme from wandering all over hell and half of Georgia for four hundred pages is quite an undertaking, for a pro or for a beginner.

I wouldn't worry too much about word-length. A publisher once told me that a book can be made to appear either short or long. It should be only long enough to tell the story. Length really isn't important, but context is.

Of course, the thing might turn out to be so lousy that My Friend, The Agent would fire it back at me, and tell me to stick to my God-How-I-Suffer 5,000 word Confessions that have been so good to me and for me for so long. If that should happen, so be it. I would have at least "done a book" -- and on my own, not as somebody else's ghost. And there might be ideas and scenes and dialogue in that stack of expensive hard-finish bond paper that could be used in short stories and articles. After all, what did I lose, except a lot of time?

But what if the thing should make it? What if a telephone call did come, telling me that a contract was on the way . . . .?

No, I've never "done a book" on my own. Maybe I never will. But if I do, I've got my game plan all written down, to be pulled out and dreamed over on productive-less days.

One thing, however, is for sure. I'll never seriously consider writing a book until I'm convinced that I have something worth-while to say. I'll never "do a book" just to *have written* a book. There are three basic reasons for writing a book. One, because there's something inside you that has to get out, and keeps nagging you to do something about it. Two, because somebody hires you to do it for him. Three, and probably the most important, just for the fun of it. Every book ever written had its inception in one of those three premises. Which one will be my reason, if and when, I really don't know. Of course, I've already used up one of the reasons with my ghost-writing stint. Which of the other two will one day motivate me to once more embark upon the stormy seas of novel writing I won't know until that day comes.

Maybe the seminar speakers and the literary sages are right. Maybe there is a book -- a meaningful book -- in every one of us. Maybe some day I will find myself yielding to the impulse to write *my* book. Because I have something to say that may be worth-while, helpful, pleasurable to somebody else. Maybe.

11 "Fringe Benefits" in Writing (Poetry, Greeting Cards, Fillers)

Interviewer: *Mr. McLarn, I heard you say the other night that there were certain "fringe benefits" in writing. Whatever were you talking about?*
Me: *Oh-oh! Another case of talking when I shouldn't. What I was going to say, before I thought better of it, was that there are some areas of writing that a writer gets into for sheer enjoyment, with little or no thought of making any money out of his incursions into non-commercial fantasy --*
Interviewer: *You just lost me.*
Me: *Oh, all right! I'm talking about such things as poetry, greeting cards, fillers -- stuff like that. But I really don't know enough about them to talk even to you --*
Interviewer: *Please do. I'll turn the tape off, okay? Now, tell me about your poetry writing.*
Me: *Well -- since it's off the record, all right. But it's against my better judgement.*

The reporter's question stirred up a lot of memories. Memories so long dormant that they seemed to come from another existence, from another side of me that I had all but forgotten I ever had.

Back in that "other world" of the 1930's, in the days when "depression" was a household word and "poverty" was respectable, there was a column in a local newspaper called "THE COAL BIN," conducted by a gentleman I never met, but learned to know pretty well through our exchanges in his column.

He had a whole passel of writers, most of whom wrote under fanciful assumed names -- Dooker Pooker, Keroma, Muscle Shoals, Dink Botts, Hic-Hic, Johnny Reb -- mine was L'Estrange, from Sir Roger L'Estrange who, along about the end of the 1600's said:

"Though this may be play to you,
'Tis death to us . . ."

I still have no idea of what he was talking about.

I was an avid reader of the column, particularly the "poetry," which ranged from terrible-to-good-to-excellent. I had never written a line of poetry, but those bits of verse became a sort of challenge. So one dreary Saturday afternoon at the office, the only place where I had access to a typewriter, I banged out a sticky-sweet sixteen-liner, called it THE HOUSE ON THE HILL, in which a love-sick youth tells his girl-friend that he's "built a new house, on top of a hill," and wants her to "please come and live in my house on the hill . . ."

I signed it "L'ESTRANGE" and mailed it, with no return address, to the newspaper column editor. Darned if he didn't publish it. And indicated in the column that he'd like to see more!

I read just the other day that "narrative poetry" -- poetry that "tells a story" -- is making a come-back. I guess I was writing narrative poetry then -- not knowing a darned thing about "accent, rhythm, metre and metric feet, iambics, trochiads, anapestics, dactylics," and all the other odd-sounding words practicing poets toss around so glibly in their poetry clubs. I didn't even know the difference between a "male" and a "female" rhyme! All I knew about poetry was that I liked to read words that flowed naturally and bounced merrily along, and if some of the last words of the lines happened to sound alike, so much the better. But mostly I read and wrote poetry for fun. Only for fun.

I heard about a book I didn't know existed -- a "Rhyming Dictionary." It was expensive, so I read the library copy. It told me more about poetry than I needed to know, although most of what the book said was so far over my head that I didn't understand it when I read it, and couldn't remember more than half of what I read. But perhaps some of it did rub off on me -- particularly the "words that rhyme" section.

I must have written upwards of a hundred of those little verses, all under the L'ESTRANGE by-line. Before long my fellow column contributors took notice of me; some of them even addressed verses to me -- mostly chiding me for not coming out of the closet and revealing my name -- "You tell me yours and I'll tell you mine." But in the kind of job I had at the time, a poet would have been as out of place as a fallen woman at a church picnic, so I drew my cloak of secrecy even closer around me, and hugged myself in glee every time somebody took a crack at me and my "poems" in THE COAL BIN column -- and that got to be pretty often.

Was I really writing poems? I don't know. For a "poem" is defined as "composition in verse, characterized by the imaginative treatment of experience and a condensed use of language that is more vivid and intense than ordinary prose . . ." By no stretch of the imagination could I convince myself that I was meeting the standards set up in that definition. But it finally dawned on me that what I was doing was finding an outlet for a side of myself that I didn't know I had. And, frankly, it scared the hell out of me. It still does.

I kept on writing those little sixteen-liners, never trying to sell any of them, being content to commune with that rhyming dictionary and a borrowed Thesaurus, and let my imagination have full sway, secure in my jealously guarded anonymity. I didn't kid myself into thinking I was a poet. I just wanted to have fun. And I did. For a long time. Until the inevitable job transfer came along, and the time I had devoted to writing my little verses fell prey to my new job demands. So, with a certain sadness in my words, I wrote my last piece for THE COAL BIN. As best I can remember, it went something like this:

"I've said my farewells to my house on the hill,
Where we spent all those gay, happy years.
With the bright yellow ducks all over the wall,
Where we laughed at our worries and fears.
But we can't plan our lives to do as we please,
For the Mills of the Gods slowly grind.
So I've shouldered my pack and taken the road
That will leave our hill-house behind.
But I've taken along, in the back of my head,
The plan of each precious room.
The tiny front porch, the funny front yard,
The climbing rose' sweet perfume.
For some day I'll find the right kind of a hill,
A hill that's just made for we two.
And I'll build a new dream house, just like the one
I lived in so long -- with you . . ."

So ended my "poetic" career. But there's a sequel to this story. Several years ago I was casting about for an idea for an original Christmas card, and ran across the scrap book in which I had accumulated the tear sheets of the poetry columns in which my verses had appeared. As I read the faded, yellowed clippings, I felt transported back into my life as it had been forty years before, and I once more renewed acquaintance with myself as I had been then.

I picked out what I considered the best of that collection, had a friend design a cover page, and another friend who ran an offset printing business "brought out" my collection, which (naturally) I titled THE HOUSE ON THE HILL. I used the book as a Christmas card. Since then I've had so many requests for it that it's now in the third printing.

If I can write verse, even *poetry*, I like to think that anybody can. I did -- but not commercially. I like to remember that when I was writing my "rhythmatics," I was giving expression to something that was imprisoned within me, and might never have emerged into the light of day if I hadn't stumbled onto that COAL BIN column.

If I'm ever asked what my formula for writing light verse is, I think I will say that it is taking every day words and situations and putting them into the kind of fanciful wordage we all have buried inside us, and hesitate to let anybody know it. For example, you might write something like this:

"When I look into your face
Time stands still . . ."

when what you really mean is, "Honey, your face would stop a clock!"

Or if you like to get satiric --

"No matter how
I slaughter thee;
The Court says thou
Shalt not kill -- me!"

That one almost got me thrown out of a political meeting.

Do you like blank verse? Try this one-

"Long years ago, in Salem Town
They burned a witch

Because a child ran shrieking through the streets
'She was singing to the moon!'
'Tis well, my love, that we lived not
Long years ago, in Salem Town.
Last night we were singing to the moon
Together . . ."

Sure you can write poetry -- or call it "verse," if it makes you more comfortable. All you need is a rhyming dictionary, a Thesaurus, and maybe a "Word Finder." Take a few of your everyday thoughts, and get romantic about them. Write down what comes into your mind. Have fun -- and look in WRITER'S MARKET for the magazines that publish verse. They may not pay much money, and some of them will pay you off in free copies. So what? You'll see your name in print, and experience the once-in-a-lifetime thrill of having somebody write you and ask you how to go about writing the way you do. You can't get much more of a fringe benefit than that. Believe it . . .

> **Interviewer:** *My! Weren't you the romantic! Did you ever try writing greeting cards? You could have.*
> **Me:** *I never wrote verse commercially, in any way. Besides, greeting cards never were my cup of tea -- even though zillions of them are written and sold every year.*

No, I never tried greeting card writing. But I'm told it's an interesting, lucrative field; that anybody with a gift for light verse, and a heart filled with sentimentality, can be quite a success in that field. I don't pretend to advise on something I don't know much about, so the only suggestion I make is for you to look at the greeting card section of a good writing directory, one of which is, of course, WRITER'S MARKET. The current issue has several pages about greeting card writing, including an excellent commentary on the subject, a glossary of the terms professionals use in discussing the greeting card business, as well as a list of the more prominent companies buying greeting cards today. I certainly couldn't improve on what the article says, and I commend it to anybody who is interested in writing the kind of material the cards contain.

I tried to find one to give to my wife on our fiftieth anniversary. I couldn't find one specifically for a husband to give his wife. Maybe not enough of us make it that far!

I wish I could tell you more about that field, but I just don't know that much more.

> **Interviewer:** *All right, we'll concede that you're not an authority on greeting cards. How about "fillers?"*
> **Me:** *Same difference. What I know about fillers could be put on the head of a pin, and leave margins.*

All I know about "fillers" is that they're those little squibs of totally unrelated information editors use when a column runs out and leaves some white space at the end. They can be just about anything; a commentary on the care and feeding of camels, when Halley's comet will be back, a hoary joke, even a brief bit of verse -- just about anything that will *fill* an aching void. They are rarely more than a couple of hundred words long, and can be as short as two lines. I've seen fillers that were taken straight out of the World Almanac, the encyclopedia, Captain Billy's Whiz-Bang -- practically everywhere. I've also seen a lot of original fillers, but I've never had the slightest interest in writing them.

If you want to try this field, WRITER'S MARKET lists a goodly number of publications that use fillers. Pick out a few of them, and do a bit of "role-playing." Imagine yourself in the editorial room of a good-sized magazine or paper, with a deadline coming up and a glaringly empty space at the bottom of one of your pages. With that grisly picture in mind, write something -- out of your head or out of your memory that will fill up that empty space. If you think of something you've seen in print, don't use it word for word, but re-write it in your own words -- especially if it comes out of an encyclopedia. The more original it can be, the better. You might get paid. Ten dollars is a pretty fair price for an original filler. Who knows? Maybe you can expand a filler into a full column. Just because I didn't write fillers is no reason why you shouldn't. They're just part of the fringe benefits in the business of writing.

I recall the night the interview-lady mentioned, when I slipped up and got myself involved in the fringe benefit business. When my listener asked me later what "fringe benefits" were, I think my answer went something like this:

"In the business world, a fringe benefit is anything of value given an employee in addition to his salary or wages, such as insurance, pension, etc. In the writing business, a fringe benefit is something writers do that they don't have to do, but do it just for the heck of it. Such as poetry. Such as greeting cards. Such as fillers. And such as anything else that puts *fun* ahead of *money . . .*"

12 "This is My Best" ("A Time for Remembering")

Interviewer: *Mr. McLarn, what do you consider as the best thing you ever wrote?*
Me: *I'll have to cop out on that one with what Browning said: "The best is yet to be . . ." I hope.*

Having too many times had the unnerving experience of throwing something away, and spending the next ten days wishing I hadn't, I never scrap anything any more. So as I prowl through that yellowing accumulation of carbon copies and tear sheets of jobs that made it and rejects that didn't, I relive portions of my life that I had forgotten -- along with some I wish I could forget.

Poring over that mass of material never fails to stir up a lot of assorted memories, along with one firm conviction. Articles that had so long ago been strictly fact-written, meticulously researched, by-the-book documented down to the last comma, make little impression on me. But those that had "come from the heart" are still just as alive, just as interesting, just as exciting as they were the day they flowed so effortlessly from my typewriter. Those are the *very personal articles.* They're not just literary exercises, banged out to order for some nit-picking editor, rushed into the mail to get a little bread for the next car payment. They're me. Jack Clinton McLarn, Human Being.

My last railroad job involved a lot of dealing with sharp, smooth office equipment salesmen. No "big deals" were negotiated, but the jumps those characters put me over gave me a post-graduate course in human nature. Personally, I couldn't sell ice-water in hell at a discount, but by the time those guys finished with me, I was a sales expert -- but from the buying side of the desk. They made me into one.

Out of my incursion into the world of professional salesman came an article titled MY FRIENDS, THE SALESMEN. When it was published, under my by-line, title, and company address, the balloon went up. Letters, calls, from salesmen, sales managers, purchasing officers, personnel managers, sales training specialists, came pouring in. Some castigated my article, my ancestry and me unmercifully. Others went into ecstasies, lauding my expose of "selling tricks and tactics." Some went so far as to gleefully relate similiar experiences. Others even said they wanted me to participate in their in-house training programs.

One irate caller, however, promised to call my boss and get me fired.

While trying to select one piece of work that I could consider as being in the This-Is-My-Best category, I found myself leaning toward MY FRIENDS, THE SALESMEN as being a pretty fair example of article writing. However, when I finished my survey, I was looking at the tear sheet of an article that brought out a side of me that neither I nor my associates ever dreamed I possessed. It gave me a new insight into my own make-up. And what it did to my image of myself as a tough-minded, no-nonsense, completely-realistic railroad man, acquired over nearly fifty years . . . well, I'll never really know.

A TIME FOR REMEMBERING was written, in first and only draft, in a Pullman roomette, on a train winding leisurely through the Carolina hills, amid the breathless beauty of a Carolina spring, with the flat, uninspired *blat* of a diesel locomotive horn striving vainly to imitate the confident, arrogant, heart-stirring chime whistle of a heavy Pacific giant of another day that the slopes of the Blue Ridge will never hear again. It was written with a huge lump in my throat, and unacustomed tears in my eyes.

I wrote it for myself, with no intention of selling it, or even showing it to anybody. But no writer can really write for himself alone. So, many months later, I sent it to an old friend, the editor of one of the few "Rail-Fan" magazines still published, just for him to read, and to perhaps remember with me the man whose writings we had known for so long -- writings of railroading as we had known it, as it "used to be."

The editor's reply was, "Jack, I shouldn't buy this, but I can't resist it. It ought to be published and will be."

It was published. People who read "Rail-Fan" magazines are a pretty sentimental lot. The letters that came to the magazine, and to me, were overflowing with movingly beautiful tributes to the man none of us had ever seen yet who had made the romance of railroading as it once was very, very real.

Here it is, just as it appeared in print.

"A Time For Remembering . . ."

As originally published in TRAINS MAGAZINE *February, 1968*

I never really "knew him." Nor did I ever see him, except in a newspaper photographer's shot of a slight, grey little man, in the high window of a steam locomotive cab, his arm lifted in the engineman's traditional salute; a grin-lighted, rugged, weathered face, the little sun-and-wind-born crevices crimping the corners of his eyes -- the indelible stamp of years of "watching ahead."

But I shall never forget him.

A good many years ago I had a railroad story in one of the men's magazines. Editors are pretty skittish about railroad yarns -- particularly when steam locomotives are concerned. They have good reason to be. There are about ten thousands of "railroad buffs," within and without the industry, notably the "model railroaders," who avidly peruse every line, fact or fiction, printed about railroading past and present, and they know their railroading with frightening accuracy.

These folks take savage delight in pouncing upon any printed blunder about any phase of railroad operation or tradition, and the editor of the magazine containing the foul-up is deluged with letters ranging from the whimsical to the downright abusive. When this happens, the author receives a chilly editorial communication enclosing the gripes. It is up to the author to justify the real or fancied goof, eat underdone crow, or try some other field of writing.

But this tale attracted surprisingly few brickbats, and a letter from one Ernest F. Weekes, which the obviously surprised editor sent to me for follow-up. While Mr. Weekes didn't exactly go overboard about the yarn, he did tell the editor that the story " . . . had more real railroading in it" than he had read for a long time.

Fan-mail to a free-lancer being something akin to manna from heaven, I immediately wrote "Ernest F. Weekes," air-mail-special. I wish I could find my copy of that letter. It was as near to a life story as I will ever write.

Soon I had a reply from "Ernie" Weekes. It, too, was a "life story." He was a locomotive engineer, with the Grand Trunk Western. He was looking forward to retirement, so he could devote full time to -- railroad-story writing!

I suppose we formed a "mutual encouragement society" then and there. That first published railroad story of mine had been hard to write, harder to sell, despite the sage admonitions of the "writing books" to "write what you know." Having spent my entire working life in the business, I do know my railroading. But I know, too, that had it not been for that first "fan letter," and those that followed, I would never have made a serious effort to write another railroad story.

We began to check on one another. There was a marked difference in our work. I wrote strictly rough-and-ready style -- tough train masters, tougher superintendents, hard-rock crewmen. The misunderstood-abused-guy-who-saves-the-train stuff. Pulpy violence and heavy-handed action. It sold, too -- all the way up to the POST.

Each sale was faithfully and gloatingly reported to Ernie. Back would come his neatly typed criticisms. Some of them were complimentary, and I would delight in his approval. But sometimes there were unhidden barbs:

"Sloppy railroading here, McLarn. But I guess it could happen on that wooden-axle pike you work for . . . A number two scoop on a heavy Pacific? We fire our basement furnaces with them out here! . . . How the heck are you going to move four trains in two directions on a single track with one 19-order? Read your rule book, bub! . . . Aw, come on! You don't let engineers sock superintendents with Stilsons and stay in service -- even if they've got it coming!"

There was one postal card he sent me that I'll always treasure. It was a comment on the story of a young train dispatcher's spine-tingling ordeal following a near fatal error in a train order. This time Ernie wrote, in his precise, firm hand:

"Whatever they paid you for this one, it wasn't enough . . ."

Soon I began to see his by-line -- over gentle, sensitive little stories in the small magazines -- church publications, Sunday school papers, juveniles. He, too, reported his sales to me, and I looked for the yarns.

For the next couple of years we had a lot of fun. But the difference between us was evident. My strictly-for-money efforts were aimed at the big circulations, and then the anthologies. Ernie stuck to his family publications, and to his theme of gentleness and understanding. His sales weren't spectacular, but they were constant and predictable. Mine weren't.

When retirement caught up with Ernie, his letter to me about his traditional "last paid trip as engineer" was a classic. The GTW, he wrote, decorated his engine until it resembled a circus wagon. (And there is no more romance in railroading?) General officers, high and low brass, came down to see him off on his last run. More met him at the other terminal. Section men, station agents, clerks along the line, all stood by as he thundered past, to wave him on. At one industrial plant there hung a sign twenty feet long -- "GOOD LUCK ERNIE WEEKES" it read -- with the factory workers lining the right-of-way fence and leaning from windows to wave Godspeed to the man they had never known, but with whom they had had a waving acquaintance for years.

Railroads are not famous for letting their people stay in one place. The word came down; I was transferred to what could be called a "roving assignment." My personal life became company life, and my writing slacked off. I still saw Ernie's work, but my comments had to be postcarded -- scribbled around hotels, in repair track offices, on trains and airplanes, whenever I found the time. And finally, that last Christmas, there was only an exchange of greeting cards. Right after the holidays, I told myself, I would write Ernie a letter.

I came home from a long trip and found an envelope bearing the familiar return address. I felt a twinge of remorse. I would read his letter, then I would sit down and write him one of the old, long-winded "visits." There was an idea for a story that would be right down his alley --

The typing was from Ernie's ancient machine. But it wasn't Ernie's letter. It was signed by his two boys. "Mr. McLarn -- this is the one that we never want to write . . ."

Ernie was gone. Quickly, quietly, just as he had so often told me he would want it. Just as he had lived.

No, I didn't "know" Ernie Weekes. Not in the conventional sense. Yet I think we *knew* each other intimately. And I think, too, that something of each of us rubbed off on the other. For now, as I read over his work and mine, I see that his characters had become a little less perfect, a little more realistic. And I was drifting away from my old Hard-Charlie types, and my people were becoming more sympathetic and believable.

Ernie had spotted this, too. One of his last comments was about a young superintendent I used as a stock character:

"Your superintendent must be growing up. He's not all hard-rock any more -- sort of in-between. Wouldn't mind at all having him in my cab . . "

Maybe it's that I'm mellowing, too. For now I think I can write a story that should be told. A story of a grey, kindly, smiling little man, framed in the high window of a vanished symbol of the age of steam, his hand resting upon the throttle of a hundred tons of controlled fury, his keen eyes unfaded by a lifetime of biting wind and blistering sun, freezing rain and searing heat.

It will be a story tailored to the needs of the small magazines that were the Literary World of Ernie Weekes. I hope it will serve as a fitting memorial to a man who, in writing to please himself, wrote his way into a host of hearts.

The story won't be mine. It will be his. For this is a time for remembering . . .

No writer should ever try to decide which of his writings are his "best." It's impossible. But if I should ever "hafta," as my grandchildren say, make such a choice, I think I would say that A TIME FOR REMEMBERING was the best I could do. Or ever will do.

Technically, professionally, I suppose A TIME FOR REMEMBERING is a fairly good example of the "Very Personal Article." It has a catchy title, a good lead, maintains a consistent mood, and has a nostalgic, if somewhat sentimental ending. It's perhaps a fair-to-middling example of a kind of writing not too much in demand among the more sensational eye-catchers on the newsstands today.

I've never gotten around to writing "The Ernie Weekes Story." Maybe I never will. But my little article was my effort to say something special to the memory of an old friend. In A TIME FOR REMEMBERING I was able to say it the only way I could say it. To say "thank you" and "so long" to an old and treasured friend, who took the time and trouble to be very kind and very helpful to a fellow railroad writer he "met" in our mutual tales of the "high iron" of another day.

13 "Do Rejection Slips Get You Down?"

Interviewer: *Mr. McLarn, I'm furious! Look what I found when I got home last night!*
Me: *Well, now! A printed rejection slip. Welcome to the club. Your first, I assume. What're you going to do with it? Frame it?*
Interviewer: *That's not funny! Of course, YOU never get them!*
Me: *Simmer down, honey. You know darned well I do. But I accept them for what they are -- an occupational hazard. And I never get one that I don't learn something from.*

The young lady who took me on as her special project was, and is, an excellent reporter. But she was, and is, a frustrated writer -- just as most of us are. And her reaction to her first formal, printed rejection slip was a traumatic experience. So was mine.

The first five pieces I wrote sold first time out. I guess they were good by the standards of those days, else they wouldn't have sold. The effect upon me, a complete novice, was earth-shaking. I visualized all sorts of things -- including quitting my cushy job, retiring to an island, and living the easy life of a selling writer. Then came Rejection Slip Number One. And punched a big hole in my balloon.

I did the usual things. Read over my five sold manuscripts. Pronounced my rejection script as good or better than any of the other five. Had my friends read them, and basked in their approval; joined with them in berating the anonymous editors for their stupidity. Conned myself into sending the same piece as was to another magazine. It came back, too -- this time without even so much as a rejection slip -- and, as a clincher, with "postage due." I hadn't put enough postage on my return envelope.

The facts of life -- the writing life -- became suddenly apparent. By means of that first printed rejection (and that return-without-a-slip) the editors taught me what rejections were -- *Learning Experiences.* Experiences that live with a writer, novice or old pro, as long as he puts words on paper, whether *for fun* or *for money*.

Rejections come in several packages. First, there is the *return unaccompanied by a printed slip.* They always made me mad -- or they did, until I queried an editor as to why she sent one of mine back "cold."

"I'm sorry," she said. "You don't need to convince me that you're a good writer. But sometimes we get scripts that we just don't like, and don't know why. Don't get your tender feelings ruffled if we don't always have time to be the nice guys."

So now, when I get one back in an otherwise empty SASE, I go over it critically, with the editor in mind from whose shop it came back unescorted. If I can't find too much wrong with it, I try it on a comparable market -- but not before doing some re-evaluating. Sometimes it works.

The second category is the *printed rejection form* or card. My apple-box filing cases contain yea-many such, all reading about the same:

> "Dear Contributor: Thank you for letting us read your manuscript. We regret sincerely that it does not conform to the immediate needs of our magazines. The Editors."

This, I regret to say, is usually the form used by the "first readers"; the people who look at material that comes in "over the transom" and out of the "slush pile." Somebody has to do the dirty work, and they do it. But when you consider that many magazines receive manuscripts by the hundreds of thousands, many of them not in acceptable, Chicago Manual of Style format, poorly typed, even sometimes hand-written, badly spelled, and the like, you will understand the frustrations of the first readers (many of them writers themselves) when they look at the Monday morning stack of work before them, or the pile left over at five o'clock on Friday, wondering how they ever got into such a crazy business.

So they are strongly tempted to grab a pad of printed rejection forms, attach them to the reeking manuscripts that stand between them and their sanity, and let the United States Mail sweep them away. But, in all fairness, I know that they don't succumb to that temptation. Instead, every script that comes into an editorial office, pulp or slick, gets at least one reading. The readers are dedicated to their jobs; they live in hope that maybe, just maybe, the next script they pick up will be a "cover story," the story all readers look for; that it will earn a "well done!" from the next editor in line, and perhaps make it all the way to the "lead story" in the next issue of the magazine. They take pride in their work. Believe me, they do.

There is another plateau along the tortuous road to publication -- the *informative rejection slip.* This one goes much further than the conventional printed rejection form. One I particularly like is a full-page printed form, thanking me for letting the editors "read my creative offering," and listing some twenty-three reasons for returning manuscripts, with a space for a check-mark opposite each reason.

The reasons range from "does not win in competition with others available," "too much narration or description," "we have on hand or have published in recent years a somewhat similar story or feature," etc., to "not suited to our needs." The reasons checked for rejecting one article of mine was "do not believe it would have a strong interest appeal to many of the readers of our magazine." There was a hand-written, unsigned note on the bottom of the form. "Our editorial board did not agree, so we are rejecting it," the note read. "I feel certain it will find a home elsewhere."

The anonymous soul in the editorial shop was right. Not long afterward I sold that same article, slightly tightened up, to a top-flight children's magazine, at a rate per word I've never equalled since!

Several magazines, especially the children's books, use this "informative" type of rejection slip, which makes me want to try again to please the editors. It is the least I can do to justify the trouble they take to encourage writers they seem to think can meet their needs.

Sometimes I get a printed rejection slip, with "A near miss -- try us again" scribbled on it. Oh, sure -- other writers better than I am get them, too. But too often we don't stop to consider what the anonymous scribbler means by that cryptic note. It simply means that the reader did see a glimmer of light at the end of the tunnel; that the writer had an above-the-slush-pile amount of ability; that the piece in its present form didn't exactly meet editorial needs -- but the sender of the note knew he or she would feel guilty if a word of encouragement weren't passed along to the writer. When I receive such a note, I go over the piece line by line. Invariably I find a weakness of structure, a confusion of plot, a fuzziness of characterization, an unrealistic bit of dialogue -- little bits of business that can usually be tightened up. I correct these defects, often doing a complete re-write, and try it again with that same magazine, and others in the same field. And I've had many of these second efforts accepted following such corrective action on my part, based upon what I think the editorial shop reader had in mind when he or she decided McLarn had something in the tale rejected, but didn't want to close the door on it completely. What the reader was saying was, "You almost made it, friend.

Give it and yourself another chance!" Such kindred souls will never know how many writers they have encouraged to try a piece "One More Time." Including me.

Finally, there is what I consider the most rewarding and the most helpful of all rejections -- the *personal letter* turn-down. I wish I could photo-copy the stack of such letters I've accumulated -- what a book they would make! Such as:

> "Dear Jack. As you knew I would, I am returning this story. I have used a couple of incest stories, so I am not against the subject *per se.* However, brother and sister are too amoral for my tastes; and no matter what the subject matter, readers must always be able to sympathize for some reason with the heroine.
>
> "Development is also completely unconvincing -- again for me. And no matter what sort of story you write for me, I don't like flip or 'cute' writing -- like 'mister' and 'brat' and 'sweetie,' etc. . . ."

What is this lady telling me? That incest is okay, but not brother-sister variety, for heaven's sake! The heroine isn't the kind of gal you wanted to pal around and sympathize with. "Unconvincing" -- the cardinal sin for the confessioneer. "Cute" -- "Flip" -- well one man's *fisch* is another's *poisson* --

I keep a card on each of the editors I consider my regular "customers," and every time one of them, wittingly or not, lets me have it about some pet no-no, I note it on the card, so when I do another piece for that same editor, I know what kind of grass to stay off of.

There was this one, handwritten, in red ink:

> "Dear Jack. Actually, there really isn't anything seriously wrong with this one, but I've used so many of this type, and the story isn't particularly new or different. Also the incident with Buddy and the way he turns up is contrived. Sorry."

What is the lady saying? "Read the book, and send me something I haven't run lately. And quit 'contriving' -- moving the characters and events around in an unrealistic manner, so as to make everything come out right. . . "

> "I'm afraid our readers wouldn't understand this any more than I did. I really couldn't figure out just what Cherry was -- or, for that matter, what sort of person the 'hero' was . . ."

Translation: "Fuzzy characterization. Hero and heroine both unconvincing."

This one I consider a classic:

> "Dear Jack. What does an editor tell a regular writer when she is not crazy about one of his manuscripts, but is at a loss to explain why? She can't send a form rejection slip -- too cold and informal. She can't send it back without a comment. So . . . I guess she just sends this note . . ."

Who wouldn't want to wear out a typewriter and a set of fingers trying to please an editor like that one?

To show that some editors do think somewhat alike, here's what another editor says about the same tale:

> "I found the writing a joy to read, sparkly and very well paced. I felt, though, that the conflict wasn't well enough defined. Sally has three separate conflicts with three separate men, and the three of them don't ever seem to jell into one overall problem that readers can sink their teeth into. It's not that she's frigid, because with two out of three (which isn't bad?) she's not, and there doesn't seem to be any major source of unhappiness in her life. I would say that the situation needs clarification. I also felt that her readiness to jump into the sack with all three men makes her less than sympathetic to our readers. Thanks again for this one, and we hope to see more in the future. . . ."

This particular editor has been writing me those inspiring little notes for years. Look what she's telling me in this one. "Conflict not defined." "One overall problem not apparent." "Situation needs clarification." "Narrator less than sympathetic." With that much direction it would seem that any good writer should be able to convert this dud into the salable script she wants. Maybe I will yet, when I can get around to it.

Here's a nice one from another top-drawer editor:

> "Thanks for these two manuscripts. Regrettably, I must return them, for I feel that my female readership will be unable to identify or sympathize with the characters. While the stories are female-narrated they seem pervaded with male sensibilities. By all means do not be discouraged, and do try again. . ."

The tale sold a couple of months later, at a fairly good rate. But what the lady was telling me in her comment was that I was writing material that would probably be better for the men's magazines than for hers. Maybe she's right. There are a good many men's magazines on the stands and listed in WRITER'S MARKET, and some of them pay excellent rates. I've never written for such books, but maybe I should look into them. Could be that I'm overlooking a bet.

This one was a beauty:

> " . . . Contrary to popular opinion, this editor prefers accompanying letters! The main reason we are not using your story is because we feel it is outdated. While I'm sure there are still kids living in the 'hippie pads,' it is not as prevalent as it was in the late 1960's, and even in the early 1970's . . ."

The lady was telling me that my story was "dated." But the next editor I sent it to didn't feel that way, because she sent me a nice check for it. So you never can tell.

I could go on and on with this. For instance, there was the story I wrote concerning the effect of an "estrogen deficiency" on the sex life of my narrator. The editor demanded that I get "medical confirmation" of what happened. I couldn't, without violating a couple of confidences. And when I tried to write around this impasse, another editor pinned my ears back with: "Accuracy in medical and other matters is your responsibility, Mr. McLarn. Sure, I could check with my own doctor, but I won't do it. That's your job . . ."

Roughly translated, she was saying, "Know your facts before you use them, and stay out of fields you know nothing about." And she was so right. I scrapped the yarn.

Reviewing these rejections and recalling my experiences with the editors who so graciously wrote them has been a delightful experience -- although some of them did leave me a bit red-faced at my own naivete. But what touched me deeply was that the editors in this business, particularly those in the "Confessex" area, were so interested and so helpful in encouraging writers. To them I shall be forever grateful.

Do rejection slips get you down? Don't let them. Instead, consider them as pithy little text-books, from which you will learn more and more about the profession you have chosen to enter. Put aside your pride, your pre-conceived ideas and convictions, and take a realistic look at what the "rejector" is trying to do. That harassed individual, usually with a stack of scripts on the desk and a deadline to meet, is extremely human. That person knows what must be done, and tries to do it. But at the same time, the editorial reader doesn't want to discourage someone who might have the potential for being a successful writer by delivering the final blow that makes a wavering writer smash a typewriter and go out and get a job as a waitress or a car wash roustabout. So he or she does the only thing possible -- sends the script back with a rejection slip, hoping devoutly that the writer will take the trouble to try to find out why it came back, and maybe try again.

If you will be objective; if you will study your rejects objectively; if you will try to recognize and not repeat the defects that trigger those rejections, you will be learning your craft from the experts. And chances are that you will find the printed rejection slips arriving with less and less frequency, personal notes coming more and more often, and the checks -- ah, those nice, nice checks -- cluttering up your mail.

May it be so. For you. And for me.

14 "Writers Make Lousy Lecturers"

Interviewer: *Mr. McLarn, haven't you been one of the lecturers at the Tar Heel Writer's Roundtable a couple of times?*
Me: *Well . . . yes, I suppose I do some speaking, but I probably shouldn't. Writers, especially me, make lousy lecturers. . .*

I never did like to stand up and talk. Even in school, I concentrated on the courses that required little recitation, to the exasperation of my teachers. Written work presented no problem for me; it was the oral quizzes that kept me out of the straight-A category. One of my teachers told my mother that compared to me, Cal Coolidge was a blabbermouth.

By the time I was in my forties I had worked myself up into a pretty good job, one that didn't require much talking, and gave me time to pursue the interests not related to my work that I had acquired along the way -- music, composition, writing. It was a pleasant sort of life, nobody bothered me much, and I guess I enjoyed it.

I would probably have enjoyed it all the way to retirement, had it not been for a young staff officer in the only company I ever worked for. One week-end he summoned me to the headquarters office, and told me abruptly that I was to organize a new department, one involving a lot of pretty rugged people in a dozen widely separated cities and towns on the system, and to run that department. Period.

When I got my breath back, and he quit talking, I started. I told him I didn't have the education, I didn't have the experience, the qualifications -- and I couldn't talk on my feet --

"Knock it off, McLarn," the young executive quirked an eyebrow at me. "I hear you saying that you don't want the job because you're scared to talk. I know your reputation as 'The Quiet Man.' It's a put-on, and you know it. Get out of here. You start Monday."

Going home on the train (there were lots of passenger trains then) I lay awake all night. Along about daylight things began to make sense. The young executive knew all about me. He had had the personnel department check me out. He knew I never opened my mouth unless I had to. Yet he had enough confidence in me to take a chance with me, put me on a pretty important job. Was it possible that he could be right? Was my "loner" demeanor only a pose? Or was it an indication that I was lacking in the guts department?

In that stuffy Pullman roomette that night, I think I got acquainted with the guy I really was for the first time. I don't think I liked what I saw.

Until that moment, for too many years I had permitted one single characteristic out of the many in my make-up to become the dominant factor of my whole existence. It had taken the discernment of one man to jar me out of what I had made for myself, a deep, comfortable rut -- the acceptance of things as they were, rather than exerting the effort it would take to make them what they could and should be.

I took the job. Not that I had much choice. Nobody passed up any kind of promotion in the organization but once. It wasn't easy to discard the crutch I had been leaning on for so long, to stop using my lack of fluency of speech as a ready alibi for not accepting responsibility.

So I took the job. And there were times when I regretted it. There were times when I found myself all but inarticulate. Sometimes I still do, even now. But in those first few weeks, as I stood before the men who were looking to me for guidance in the new way of doing things in the new department, I suddenly realized that they weren't even thinking about *how* I was expressing myself. They weren't expecting the skilled oratory, the glib, well-turned phrases of a Lionel Barrymore or an Adlai Stevenson. They were listening for *what* I was saying, not *how* I was saying it. They didn't care -- not in Memphis or St. Joe, Natchez or Mobile. They were looking to me for instruction, for counsel, for help. They gave not a damn how I helped them, just so I did it.

I kept that job, and others like it, all the way to my retirement from the industry in which I spent my entire working life. And if that nice interviewer were to ask me today about my "lecturing activities," I don't think I would be quite so flippant in answering her.

Yes, I do some lecturing -- but not always as a professional. Sometimes I talk informally to dedicated writing groups, such as the Tar Heel Writer's Roundtable, about my experiences as a free-lancer. Sometimes to management and sales personnel, on business subjects. Once in a while on religious topics, bible study -- and I even teach a men's Bible class. But the most rewarding audiences I ever have are the kids.

A few years ago I had several stories published in children's magazines. So many, in fact, that a fourth grade county school teacher called me to ask if I would talk to her class about "how you write for children."

I had instant misgivings. What could I say to fourth graders that would interest them? At first I begged off, but the lady was persistent and persuasive, she said there would only be about fifteen in the class, so I finally accepted. After all, fifteen kids couldn't do me much damage.

When I reached the school that morning, I got a rude shock.

Instead of fifteen kids, the whole fourth grade section of the big county school was in the assembly room to hear me! I had never seen so many scrubbed up youngsters in one place in my life. Some of them eyed me with ill-concealed hostility. As I was introduced others snickered behind their hands, ignoring the admonishing looks of the teachers who were sprinkled among them, with "don't-you-dare-move!" written all over their faces.

I managed to get my talk going. I told them how I started writing for children, how I found my plots, how I did my writing. And all at once I sensed a thawing of the chill air of the assembly room. I was getting through to them! Happily, I relaxed, and before I realized it, I wasn't making a talk, I was just telling a bunch of kids about my daughter, and how I told my "'tories" to her. I was telling them about my three grandchildren, "who were once just your ages." It was fun -- especially when I climaxed my talk by reading them one of my railroad stories, about a ten-year-old boy who knew how to telegraph, and because he did know, saved a train from disaster. The kids literally ate it up. And when I brought out of my brief case the ancient telegraph key and sounder my father had used to teach me the Morse code when I was ten, more than a half-century ago -- they fairly squealed.

When I finally reached the end of my presentation, the kid's applause brought tears to my eyes. Maybe they were applauding because they didn't have to do anything for a half-hour or so. I don't know. But I do know that never before had I had a more attentive and apparently appreciative group of listeners.

Since then I have talked to many fourth and fifth graders, once upon the invitation of a lad from next door -- one of my "honorary grandchildren" with which my neighborhood has somehow become filled. I gave much the same talk to that group, and darned if the whole class didn't line up to get my autograph! And a week later I received "thank you" letters from a dozen of the kids.

But what touched me most was one big-eyed little girl sidling shyly up to me and saying, "Mister, I liked your story a whole lot." She was so like another big-eyed little girl who said, so long ago, "Daddy, you tell the *goodest* 'tories . . ."

Sure, I do some "lecturing." According to the "Speakers' Manuals," I do it wrong, completely.

I forget to button my jacket, if I'm wearing one.

I make reference to how much better the preceding speaker was than I'm going to be.

I put my hands in my pockets. If I don't I cling to the lectern with the same white-knuckled intensity I exercise on airplane seat armrests, or lean on it in a way that makes me look not unlike the Hunchback of Notre Dame.

When I speak from cards, I manage to get them mixed up, or drop them. If I use a prepared manuscript, I skip words and lines, get lost. I've never yet completed a talk without going off on a tangent and winding up talking about something completely unrelated to the topic I was supposed to discuss.

In spite of all these boo-boos, I get invited back, so I must be doing something right.

Why do I go to all the trouble to make talks? I don't really know. Maybe it's because we all have a lot of the "ham" in us, and I have an over-supply of that commodity. Maybe it's because I'm remembering a not-too-happy youngster who found himself in a hostile world that had little place for him, and because I'm trying to make up to that kid for letting him down during all those formative years. Maybe -- I just don't know.

Sometimes I get "honorariums" from those speaking engagements. Mostly I don't. Lately I've had to decline some of them -- distance, gas restriction, weather, health, whatever. But there are some invitations I never decline. Invitations to speak to kids. Of any age. Not just to "speak about writing," but to talk, to "rap" about anything the kids want to hear and argue about. To say to them, as only an old man can say it, "Look, you guys, it's not the way you talk, but what you say that counts. Take it from one who's been where it's at, okay?"

I learned that the hard way. Sure, I'm a lousy lecturer, but maybe I can make it a little easier for the kids to learn the same thing.

15 What is a Successful Writer?

Interviewer: *Mr. McLarn, as a successful writer --*
Me: *Me? Successful? No way. A successful writer has to work like hell to be successful, and harder to stay that way. Sure, he makes a lot of money, but he doesn't have much fun doing it. Me, I work only when I want to. I don't try to make a lot of money writing but I do have a whale of a lot of fun doing it. A successful writer? Not me --*
Interviewer: *Please, Mr. McLarn, be serious! You know I can't put anything like that in this interview!*
Me: *Honey, it's downright impossible for me to take anything seriously for more than about thirty seconds. Least of all myself . . .*

When the somewhat miffed young lady took herself and her tape recorder off my patio, I was a bit ashamed of myself. After all, she had done me a favor. I had learned a whole lot more about me from her than she had learned about me from me.

That afternoon while mowing the lawn I did a little more serious thinking than is my usual wont. About writing. And about what "writing success" really meant -- to me -- to anybody.

In the brochure for a Writer's Roundtable at which I was among the several speakers, the director billed me as a "successful fiction and technical writer." Gratifying. At least, it was gratifying until one of my wise-guy grandsons got hold of the thing. After snickering over it for a while, he said, "Gran'daddy Jack, it says here you're a 'successful fiction and technical writer.' What does that mean? I thought you were just a retired railroad man. How did you ever get to be a 'successful writer'?"

Leave it to a smart-alec kid.

I floundered around for a little while and came up with this gem of wisdom. "A successful writer is one who beats his brains out writing stories for kids like you."

That answer didn't satisfy him any more than it satisfied me.

According to Sam Clemens, we come into this world unwillingly. Certainly we do not ask to be born into it. But once we are here, most of us manage to make out as best we can, for so long as God permits. We live "one life, in one world . . ."

In our scheme of things, perhaps "one life, one world" should be enough. But somehow they weren't enough for me. And because they weren't enough, I consider myself one of the luckiest characters ever. For I've had the rare privilege of living -- and enjoying to the fullest -- two completely different lives, in two completely different worlds.

For nearly fifty years one of those two worlds was the world of heavy industry; a world in which the word "success" meant how much money you made, what kind of cars (plural) you drove, whether your office had wall-to-wall carpeting, a wooden or a steel desk, a refrigerated liquor cabinet, a hot-line telephone to the executive floor; the kind of school your kids attended, whether they were limousined or bused there -- stuff like that.

I never made it even close to the "executive level" in that world. I spent my entire working life in that never-never land of bureaucratic mediocrity, somewhere between the big-shots who did the planning and pushed the buttons, and the hard-hat-and-calloused-hands guys who got the jobs done.

But in every job, every office I had, I felt a keen obligation to the people around me. Everywhere I went, my first concern was finding somebody to train to take my place, "if and when." Everywhere I went, I left behind me for my successor an up-to-the-last-day written record of just about everything he would run into -- every problem I had faced, every solution I had found to those problems. I tried to leave the guy an account of what I had learned about what he would learn -- my achievements as well as my mistakes mercilessly included.

I still have the note one of my successors wrote, not long after his appointment to succeed me. "Boy, did you have the old man figured! Thanks to your brief, I know when to speak and when to keep my mouth shut!"

Some of the kids who worked for me I literally dragged kicking and screaming out of their little niches, their safe, unexacting, undemanding routines, and shoved them willy-nilly toward a future they didn't know existed, and cared even less that it did exist. Some of them have already gone beyond anything I ever accomplished for myself in the way of advancement. I never had a key to the executive washroom. But some of "my kids" are going to have those coveted status symbols. And I'd bet money that a couple of them will eventually have their own private privies, which is about as high as anybody gets in that particular industry!

I did a lot of "inspirational writing" (for free) for those fellows. I like to think that some of the things I wrote may have had something to do with helping them to attain the success I didn't. Maybe I did "succeed" in other ways, when I literally drove them toward their own successes.

Just when it happened I'm not too sure, but somewhere along the way I found that there was another world. A world in which I could live another, a different life. A life of my own creation, in a world of my own making. A world in which every foot of land, every drop of water, every tree, every bush, every man, woman, boy, girl, animal, bird existed because I willed that they exist. I found the world of a writer -- the kind of a world only a writer can create. A world completely my own. A world in which I could do with everybody and everything in it just as I pleased. I could will that people be born. I could decide when they would sing, dance, laugh, weep -- even die.

True, that world was only a paper-and-typescript world, conceived in my mind, born of my fingers and the twenty-six letters of the alphabet; the hundreds of thousands of words they can form. A world of my own will, my own desire, my own purpose. But to me it was a very real world, one into which I could retreat at will, shutting out that cold, crass other world of big-business-and-making-a-living, for as long as I wanted it shut out. For as long as I wanted to be free of it.

A strange thing happened. I found that there actually were people who wanted to know about that "other" world of mine. People who wanted to know what happened to the creatures of my imagination that peopled the world. There were actually editors who would pay me for the tales of that realm of fancy into which my mind and my typewriter permitted me to enter, to remain as long as pleased me. I suppose that, too, is a form of success -- being able to produce something that people will somehow enjoy -- and maybe even think about.

The world of commerce, of business, of industry is behind me now; my ties with that world have long since been severed. All I have left of it is a host of memories -- good times, good friends, good things -- plus, of course, those nice retirement checks that brighten up the first day of the month, every month.

My "real world" today is a world in which I enjoy every shining moment. My hills and my valleys are delightfully cool and green, peopled with the generations of my imagination, ready, willing, even eager to do without question, whatever I dream up for them to do. I have the days to come to look forward to, to be spent with them, having them tell their stories through me; stories I get paid for just putting down on paper. And I believe that there will always be real people who will want to escape for a time into my world -- the world of imagination, the world of fantasy, the world of the writer, even for just a little while.

I do not think that *success* in business, in writing. in anything can be considered separately and alone. Success can really be found in but one area -- in the area of living. And success in living is not measured by swollen bank accounts, by vintage Mercedes-Benz', by any of the puny fetishes in which we put so much store. Every man, every woman, has to establish criteria for success. For what is nectar to one may bear the taste of ashes to another.

Taped to the wall above my desk is a faded, yellowing piece of paper, bearing a single involved, ungrammatical sentence I wrote many years ago as my own adolescent "definition of success." If the young lady with the tape recorder ever comes back (which she probably won't) I would like to tell her what's in that sentence.

> *"If, because of something I do, or say, or write; or do not do, or say, or write, I give someone else a moment, an hour, a day, or a lifetime with just a bit more meaning, a bit more happiness, or a bit less sadness; for that moment, that hour, that day, or that lifetime I can say, 'I have been a success'!"*

I seldom give advice, for I rarely take it. But perhaps it is not too far amiss for me to commend to you a quest, a search for your own *other* world. For your own world as a writer. If you are successful in that quest, you will find that world a mighty nice place to visit, in which to spend the most pleasantly rewarding hours you will ever know. You might have a lot of fun, too -- just as I have, and still am -- just as I hope to continue to have fun as long as I'm around to enjoy it.

I hope you find that other world. It's there. All you have to do is find the door, open it, and walk in. Who knows? You just might want to stay.

To illustrate points raised in the foregoing text, we are including in this appendix, with the permission of the copyright owners, four of the author's many published stories and articles, showing how he goes about analyzing material.

We are also including a specially prepared unpublished recording script in the format preferred by some cassette publishers; an analysis of a book review, and an example of how a manuscript is professionally prepared.

The Editor

Appendix I

How To Analyze the Confession Story

"I Can't Make Love To You, Darling!"

Editor's blurb -- not mine. Tells too much about the story.

Each time I took her in my arms, the dead face of a Vietnamese girl came between us . . .

Indication at beginning of story that narrator has a problem.

Raising my voice a little over the blasting of the jukebox and still trying not to sound mad, I said into the telephone, "Listen, honey. Like I just told you, the hydraulics went out on the rig, and I jack-knifed just out of River City -- tied up the Freeway for an hour. I got towed to the terminal here, but it'll be tomorrow before I can get rolling again. I'm sorry as hell --"

My wife's voice, sweet, patient, resigned, as it always was, came from five hundred miles away. "I'm sorry, too, darling," she said. "But I know you can't help it. At least nobody is shooting at you. I hear music -- where are you?"

"In a crummy little bar-and-grill near the truck terminal," I said. "It's raining, cold -- a lousy way to spend an anniversary -- "

"Don't worry about it," she said. "Call me when you start home." Again that matter-of-fact, everything's-all-right tone. "Don't drink too much, okay? 'Bye."

"Katie, wait!" I said. "I want to tell you that I love you --"

The line buzzed emptily. I banged the instrument down, once more anger -- and something else -- sweeping over me. Damn it, if she had only gotten mad -- yelled at me -- cried -- or something to show that not being together on our third anniversary meant disappointment, it would have been different. But that gentle, tolerant acceptance was hard to take.

The jukebox fell silent. I put a couple of quarters into it, pushed the buttons without looking at them, wandered back to the bar. The place was all but deserted. A girl was sitting on a stool at the other end of the bar, a drink in front of her, a cigarette drooping from her lips.

(Character planted, to be used later.)

"Martini," I said to the bartender. "Make it a double."

"Never order a double, friend," the man grinned. "You'll get a one-and-a-half instead. I'll fix you a couple of singles to start."

He went about making drinks, the juke box blared into life. As the first notes of the bittersweet song about love and lost love poured from the machine, I gritted my teeth. Why did it have to be that song? The same song that came from our bedside radio that night in Honolulu, where Katie had met me for my "rest and recreation" leave a year ago -- leave from the stench of mud and blood and death that was Viet-Nam. The night we both found that Katie didn't have a husband any more --

Identification of problem -- sexual impotence.

only a six-foot-three carcass of a man, whose seemingly powerful body was helplessly unable to respond to the love she had come so far to offer . . .

Flash-back, bringing story up to date.

I had met Katie at a dance at the USO a month before I was due to ship out. She was wearing a skimpy, tight dress and a tighter sweater. Her dark hair tumbled in a cloud about her shoulders as she danced, flirting gaily with all of us. Half the guys in the place made a play for her -- including me -- but she was like a cricket -- you just couldn't catch her in one place long enough to make a really effective pitch.

After a while I drifted into the bar next door to the USO, had a couple of beers, and started down the street to get the bus back to the base. Then I saw her come out. She was alone -- and seemed to be looking for somebody. When she saw me, she smiled.

"Hi!" she said. "Where did you disappear to? I was looking for you."

"For what?" I groused. "You were doing all right. And that outfit you're wearing --"

"Like it?" she giggled. "It's my kid sister's, and it fits -- well . . . I'm really a square," she went on. "So much so that I'd like a malted. Want to buy me one? -- Sergeant Roy Crider, I see by your name plate." She wrinkled her nose at me. "I'm Katie Novak."

We had a malted. It was late when I walked her home, to a big old house on a dark side street. There was an old-fashioned lawn swing in the yard, just like the one we had back home in Illinois. It creaked a welcome as we sat down. I was feeling good and relaxed, and she didn't seem to mind when I put my arm around her -- except that she did tense up a bit.

When I kissed her, she shivered. There was a catch in her voice as she said, "Ooh! Do you work fast! But you are sort of -- nice." She lifted her lips again, and I began to enjoy the warm glow that was creeping over me.

Teaser Sex Scene

It wasn't long before my hand found her breast. She shook her head without freeing her lips from mine, pushed my hand away. Her tight dress was hiked up -- invitingly, I thought. I caressed her knee, let my hand creep up her thigh, seeking the bareness above her stocking. A shudder ran through her, sending the blood leaping through me. I pulled her closer. She turned her head, and with icy calm, said, "Don't waste your time, Sergeant. They're panty hose."

Her tone startled me. But I laughed. "Aw, come on, honey," I said. "Don't spoil the party. After all, I'm going away soon -- fighting for you. So why can't we just --"

"I guess the Crusaders used that same pitch," she said, with what might have been sadness in her voice. "And it didn't work for them any better than it will for you tonight. No, Sergeant, you made a mistake. I think we both did."

Before I could move, she slipped out of my arms, pressed her lips to mine for a breathless instant. Then she was gone, into the dark house. The door closed behind her with a soft, final thud.

Narrator has second thoughts about heroine.

Shaken, I sat where I was for awhile. What had begun as a fun date, with a good chance of making-out on the side, had turned into something else. My whole body was one big ache. I could still taste her soft, warm lips on mine. I could still feel her body pressing against mine -- hear the little catch in her breath as she returned my kiss --

I finally walked back to town, just in time to miss the last bus to the base. The taxi-driver gypped me, the gate sentry gave me a hard time, and the cold shower didn't help a bit. Neither did my dreams. . .

The next evening I was at the USO again. She didn't show. So I walked to her house. It was easy to find -- she was sitting in the lawn swing, alone. Even in the dusk I saw that she was wearing something soft and flowing and white. She looked like an angel.

"Hi," I said. "You weren't there, so I thought -- "

"It wasn't my night there," she said. "Besides, last night wasn't much fun, now was it?"

I sat down across from her, her knees touched mine. The

old swing creaked as we rocked in silence. She was wearing a scent that reminded me of my grandmother's spice jar back home --

"Okay, Katie," I said. "I'm sorry about -- about -- "

"Sorry? Why? Because you didn't score? Or because you tried to?"

I felt like a tongue-tied high school boy. "Aw, Katie, don't," I said. "After the way you kissed me, I thought -- well, I guess I'll shove off -- "

"You big softie!" she laughed, a throaty little sound that made me shiver with longing. "I'd have died if you hadn't come out here tonight. Come on -- sit over here. Kiss me -- just once, darn it -- and keep those big hands in bounds. Let's start over -- from scratch, okay?"

From then on things really happened. That very night she took me in the house to meet her parents and her kid sister. A week later we spent a lot of time on the telephone, calling my folks, my commanding officer at the base -- and, finally the chaplain.

We were married in the base chapel. Our honeymoon was a week-end in a little motel down the coast.

Romantic-Sex Scene

Katie giggled as I carried her over the threshold of our motel room. "So it's funny?" I said, a little annoyed.

"I was just thinking," she said. "About the look on your face that night, when you found out about panty hose. Were you ever frustrated!"

It was a wild, wonderful weekend. The world and all that was in it became ours. Too soon it was over, and I was on an airplane, headed for Asia, with only a dozen snapshots and a lot of memories to ease the lonely ache in my heart.

Approach to problem.

On our first anniversary, I was slogging through rice paddies in one of those "search and destroy" missions too dear to the hearts of the six-o'clock news people. We were making a sweep through the delta countryside, where the 'Cong had just pulled out -- we thought. So when one of them suddenly popped out of a hole not thirty feet away, we were caught flat-footed. He got off a burst that killed two people right next to me, and vanished into a straw-thatched hut, like a rabbit into a burrow. Screaming in a sick fury, with the blood of my buddies half-blinding me, I lobbed a grenade after him, hit the deck. The hut exploded; dirt, mud, timbers rained everywhere.

When the noise died away and we moved forward, I heard a sound coming from the shattered hut. Out of the smoke and dust a figure came -- a woman. Bloody, torn, her face contorted, she screamed something in Vietnamese, collapsed in the mud and filth.

I approached her gingerly. She was little more than a child. But it was all too obvious that she was having a baby.

"Medic!" I yelled. "Get over here! On the double!"

The medic, a kid hardly old enough to shave, came running. He leaned over the girl, shook his head. "Sheesh, Sarge!" he said. "Pharmacy school didn't have much of a course in obstetrics. But I'll try."

So while the world's dirtiest war stopped, while a bunch of tough GI's stood in a protecting circle around her, the girl brought a tiny Vietnamese boy protestingly into the dirty, messed up world. The medic got to his feet, white-faced.

"The mother didn't make it, Sarge," he panted. "Sorry. Better get a chopper in for them." He indicated the green "body bags" holding what had been two soldiers I'd just had chow with an hour before. "They can take the baby and -- and her along."

He wrapped the baby in the torn, bloody pajamas the girl-mother had been wearing. I don't know why, but I just had to give the littly guy something. I unpinned my name plate, fastened it to the improvised robe.

Dawning of narrator's guilt-complex.

As the chopper fluttered down, rotors flattening the rank grass where death could be hiding, I looked for a long time at the body of the girl. The half-open eyes seemed to meet mine -- as though they were looking into my soul. I had killed her. Because of me, a little boy had been born without a chance in a million of knowing what life had to offer --

As the chopper clattered away, I lifted my arm in the gesture that is as old as war itself. "All right, you guys!" I bellowed. "Charlie's waiting! Move out!"

The days, the months that followed were sheer hell. I lived through such horrors, witnessed such incredible cruelties, and did such ghastly things myself that I sometimes wondered if I could not be in some awful nightmare, wishing desperately that I could awake to find it all a dream. And at night, in the stinking mud, the leech-infested jungles, even in the plush Saigon hotels, I would wake suddenly, aware that I had been dreaming -- but dreaming of a tiny Vietnamese girl, lying bloodily dying on the ground, while a grim-faced young giant with a blood-red cross on his helmet dragged a living infant from her body --

What if it had been the other way around? What if that had been Katie, bleeding, dying there on the filthy earth . . . while my son was being born . . . ?

Things were bad with my outfit. It was another year before my CO put in for "rest and recreation" leave for me. But finally I was waiting at Hilo when Katie's airplane touched down. I cried, because I was so glad to see her, and because she was so beautiful. We clung together so long that a grinning MP suggested that we go somewhere and not block traffic.

That night, in our room overlooking the Pacific, we had dinner sent up -- island delicacies -- champagne -- the works. She had brought a gorgeously sheer white nightie with her. She stripped shamelessly nude, put it on, smiled at me.

"No panty hose tonight, darling," she said. "Just me."

The radio was playing that bittersweet song. The country-western singer's voice was sad, as I swept Katie into my arms, put her on the bed -- lay down beside her -- her soft, warm body nestling eagerly against mine --

All at once she wasn't there! Instead, I was holding in my arms the bloody, torn, filthy body of a Vietnamese girl -- and a baby was coming from her loins --

Dramatic scene as narrator realizes his condition. Problem!

I screamed. I couldn't help it.

"Roy!" Katie cried. "What is it, darling? What's wrong?"

Frantically, I caught her to me, pressed my body against her softness, trying to shut out the hideous vision, wanting to make her body part of mine, the bodies of the living. For a long time I held her desperately -- wanting her -- trying -- oh, God -- trying to love her --

Then, in a burst of ghastly, sickened realization, I knew! I knew I couldn't make love to my wife. My body, once so eagerly responsive to even thoughts of her, had betrayed me. I was no longer a man!

I shook with sobs. For a long time we lay there, Katie's arms around me, her body pressed close, smooth, soft, warm, passionate -- her voice murmuring in soothing, comforting compassion.

"Never mind, darling," she kissed me. "I know you love me. Let's go to sleep. Tormorrow I want to buy a grass skirt -- eat a pineapple -- tomorrow night will be different -- you're just so tired --"

The few days in the island paradise were heavenly. We walked on the sand, played in the surf, tumbled off surfboards like two happy kids. We explored the streets, choked down fish and poi, went to luaus and stuffed.

But at night, in the luxurious room, in each other's arms,

the surf booming below, the steel guitars wailing love-songs -- nothing.

More than once I woke to find Katie standing by the window, the moonlight shining on her body through the gossamer gown. And when I touched her pillow, it was damp with tears . . . tears for me . . . and for my lost manhood.

Narrator's acceptance of his problem.

I hadn't been back on combat duty a month when I blundered into a Viet-Cong land-mine. By the time the doctors had dug the fragments out of my legs, my army career was over. Six months later, I was home, a civilian again, limping just a little.

Mid-Continental Freight was glad to give me my old job. Long-distance diesel jockeys were in short supply, and my injury wasn't disabling for the driving. Not my leg injuries, anyway. My worst scar didn't show up in any X-rays. It showed up where it hurt even more. In bed. In the gentle resignation, the sweet tolerant acceptance that seemed to tinge Katie's every thought of me . . .

Introduction of previously planted character to the action.

"She was sexy -- but no tramp. And she seemed to want me for a lover. Me! What a laugh! What a shock I had in store for her. . ."

(Another unnecessary editorial blurb, not mine. Action is enough!)

"Is this a private celebration, or can just anbody get in?"

I jumped. The juke-box was playing a soft, corny little melody. The two Martinis were before me, untouched -- and the girl from the other end of the bar was climbing onto the bar stool beside me.

"Get lost, sister!" I growled. She laughed -- a sad sort of laugh.

"Guess this is my drink," she said. "Thanks. My name's Nora." She tasted the Martini, made a face. "Wow!" she said. "Mike's sure laid it on this time -- twelve to one I'll bet. He must like you."

I looked at her curiously. She was young, and she would have been pretty, except for little worry-wrinkles around her too-heavily-shadowed eyes. After all, what harm was there in buying her a drink?

"Be my guest," I said. "Hey, Mike -- do this again, okay?"

"I heard you talking to your wife." The girl twirled the glass in her long fingers. "Is she pretty?"

"A doll, " I said. "Sweet, too. Too damned sweet. I'd feel better if she'd yell at me."

We sat there for a long time, just talking about nothing much. Her voice was soft, husky, refined. The plain black dress that molded her small figure so perfectly would have cost me a week's salary.

Later, after a few more of Mike's blockbusting Martinis, the girl glanced at her small, expensive-looking watch.

"Want to take off with me?" she said briskly. "I live not far from here."

I sighed. Too bad. A lovely girl like this, just another pro, looking for a cash customer.

"Forget it, honey," I said. "You wouldn't have any fun -- and I wouldn't either, believe it."

She laughed. Once more that sad little laugh.

"Don't knock what you haven't tried," she said. "Come on. Or are you chicken?"

I shrugged. "Why not?" I said. The Martinis were making me a little woozy. I paid the bartender, followed the girl out into the night.

Fog was blowing in from the river, turning the street lights into blurred white blobs. A block or so away we turned into one of the posh apartment buildings in the area. The apartment she ushered me into was small, but beautifully furnished. The girl switched on the TV, got a bottle and two glasses from a cabinet. "Work on this brandy," she said. "I'll only be a minute."

She vanished into a bedroom; I heard a shower running. The brandy was old and good, and mixed well with the Martinis. A warm glow began to spread all over me.

There was a photograph on the TV, of a man -- handsome, distinguished-looking. "Quite a girl you've got there, mister!" I lifted my glass in a mock salute. "Wish I could do her some good!"

The girl came back. She was wearing a flaring black house-coat -- and I got the sudden feeling that there wasn't anything under it but girl. She poured a glass of brandy, sat down on the sofa across from me.

"Cheers," I said. "But you're sure going to be sorry you went to all this trouble for nothing."

She didn't answer me, just glanced at her watch. I started to move over beside her -- the least I could do was go through the motions. But her look stopped me. Puzzled, I went back to my chair. She kept glancing at that watch.

"Say, if you're expecting somebody, I'd better shove off," I said, suddenly a bit apprehensive.

She shook her head. Just as the eleven o'clock news started, she put her glass down, turned the TV off. "Come on," she said. "Come with me."

I followed her into the bedroom. With no hesitancy, no coyness, she took off the house-coat. I was right. There wasn't a thing under it. She lay down on the king-sized bed.

"Put your clothes on that chair," she said. "And please hurry." Once more she looked at her watch.

Explicit sex scene.

"Nora, honey," I said. "You're not going to belive this, but -- "

I stopped in utter amazement. My body, long unresponsive to even the most appealing of sex-impulses, had suddenly come alive. Thundering, passionate urges took fierce possession of me. I fairly tore my clothes off, reached for the light switch.

"No!" the girl said harshly. "Leave it on! Hurry!"

Not believing what I was hearing, I lay down beside her. She came against me with an intensity that startled me. And then we were together, her lush body thrashing convulsively against mine. She spoke only one word, over and over -- "Give -- give -- *give!*"

And, in ecstatic relief, I responded! Again and again, until we both lay exhausted, and I could feel the thudding of her heart against my body. I had satisfied her! I was a man again!

"Nora," I whispered against her breast. "You're wonderful. I --"

"Get up." Her voice was cold. "Get out of here. Now!"

For a moment I just lay there. Then I said, "What the hell is this? You invited me, remember?"

"Of course I did," she pushed me away, got up, donned the house-coat. "Want to know why?"

"Why?" I snapped, getting into my clothes. "Money, I guess. What else? Okay -- how much?"

"Money? Hah!" I followed her back to the living room, knotting my tie. She poured a glass of brandy, handed it to me, lit a cigarette.

"Just about now," she looked at that watch once more. "Just about now my loving husband is in St. Louis, getting into bed with his latest girl friend. I never cheated on him before. But I wanted to beat him to it. Just once. Now, I have!"

"You sure have!" I gulped the brandy. "But, Nora -- I've got to tell you something --"

"Forget it!" she said. "Just get out of here. I used you to get even with my husband. But now I hate myself -- and you, too. Everything about you! Oh, get out of here! Please!

She ran into the bedroom, slammed the door. But I could

hear her crying. I let myself out, walked back to the bar-and-grill, feeling ashamed and elated at the same time. I had been born again!

"Hello again!" the bartender said as I walked in. "How'd things go?"

"Fine," I said. "Fix me another of those Martinis. And I'd like to buy you a drink."

"Never touch it," the barkeeper said. "I just sell the stuff."

Narrator thinks his experience has cured his impotence. That his "problem" is solved.

As soon as my hydraulics were fixed the next day, I took off, pushed the rig to the limit. It was a wonder I didn't get a hatful of tickets, but I was too happy to care if I did. It was late when I wheeled into the terminal, did my paper work, took a taxi home.

I was almost there when a chill struck me. How was I going to tell Katie? What could I tell her? A guy doesn't come barging in and tell his wife, "Look, honey, there was this broad in River City. Guess what --"

I groaned aloud. I couldn't tell her. I couldn't hurt her any more than I already had. Not Katie.

She opened the door, hugged me. She was wearing the baggy pajamas I hated.

"Oh, I've missed you so much!" she said. "The neighbors came over last night. We got some wonderful anniversary gifts -- darling, is something wrong?"

"Katie," My voice was shaking, and so was I. "Sleep with me tonight."

"Sleep with you? But, honey --" a sudden light glowed in her eyes. "Oh, yes! I'll go put on a nightie."

I hurried through my shower, as excited as I had been on my wedding night. Everything was going to be all right. Had to be all right!

Katie was already in bed when I came out of the shower. Her slim body glowed white through the sheer gown -- the same gown she had worn that awful night in Hawaii. Lord, she was beautiful. I reached for her --

Narrator finds that he is still impotent. With his wife.

Then it was midnight. I was lying with my arms behind my head, staring at the ceiling. Katie was beside me, her body quivering. She wasn't crying. Because she couldn't cry any more.

"Darling, darling!" she quavered. "I can't take any more of this. I just can't Please do something. See a doctor. You're killing both of us!"

I didn't answer her. I was thinking about a lot of things. A dying woman and a new-born infant . . . that night in Hawaii . . . the strange girl in the big bed in River City. . . my passionate interlude with her . . . my service automatic in the bureau drawer . . .

No. Katie didn't have that coming.

"Okay," I muttered. "Tomorrow. Tomorrow I'll do something. But God only knows what!"

She kissed me. Then, like a tired child, she went to sleep in my arms. But I didn't dare close my own eyes. I didn't dare face the dreams I knew would come. . .

Narrator tries to solve his problem through outside help.

It took more than one visit to the psychiatric clinic to which the company doctor sent me. More than once the sessions would end with the psychiatrist and me shouting at each other. When the visits were over, I felt as though I had been drained of all vitality, reduced to a miserable hunk of nothing.

The doctor was no punch-puller. "It's not uncommon," he told me, "for a returning service man to feel guilty about what he did in combat. Most of them throw it off in time. Others can't. You, for instance."

"I don't see much help in talking into that damned tape recorder," I said. "What good does it do to rehash all that stuff? If I'm mentally sick, why don't you just put me away?"

"Idiot," the doctor grinned. "It doesn't do any good except to give us an idea of what makes you tick. For instance, it's already told us that when you accidentally killed that woman, you bought yourself one hell of a bunch of guilt. You judged yourself, tried yourself, convicted yourself and sentenced yourself by denying yourself the one thing you valued most -- your wife's love, represented by her body.

"You also told us that you put your wife in that woman's place. You saw *her* lying there. You saw *her* dying. You saw *your* son being born. And you couldn't take it. So --"

"Wait a minute!" I said. "That woman in River City. Why -- how could I do what I did with her, and not with my wife? Answer me that, doctor!"

"I don't condone immorality," the doctor said. "But in your case it was fortunate. That woman wasn't connected with the past. The guilt within you didn't recognize her at all. So you reverted to your old, virile self. Well, that's all we can do for now. Any suggestions?"

He shut the recorder off. A strange feeling was creeping over me -- as though an answer was struggling with the question within my agonized mind.

"I'll have a full report by the end of the week," the doctor said. "We can begin therapy then. It may do some good -- "

"Thanks, doctor," I said. "I've got a sort of idea of my own."

Narrator determines to help himself.

It took a long time. Months of digging through army and civil records, State Department records. Hours of interviews with bored bureaucrats. Up and down the blind alleys of big government, facing one frustration after another -- searching for one pitiful little boy in the incredible confusion of a war-ravaged land. It took all the time I could spare from my job and a lot of money, too. Through it all, Katie was at my side, her quiet serenity many times making bearable the disappointments I met at almost every turn.

But at last Katie and I stood waiting as the huge transport airplane touched down, and a lieutenant-nurse came down the ramp, carrying a small Vietnamese boy.

When I reached the ramp, I saw something on his jacket. My name plate! CRIDER, ROY A! He didn't know me. How could he? But when his eyes met mine, his moon-like face lighted up in an infectious grin.

"Hi, son!" My eyes were filled with tears as I reached for him. "Welcome home!"

But Katie was ahead of me. She took the boy from the nurse. "I think, daddy," Katie said. "That our son wants to go to the bathroom."

Final solution of problem.

That was two years ago. Now "Kim", no longer a curiosity in the community, gets into and out of mischief with a serene regularity that exasperates Katie and delights me.

No. When we brought him home, it didn't all at once solve everything. I didn't become "normal" overnight. Rather it took long hours of therapy, tedious sessions at the clinic.

But one night, when we had both been up ministering to one small boy with one big stomach-ache following a birthday party, Katie in her baggy pajamas and her hair in curlers, me a little bleary-eyed and grumpy, our bodies just happened to touch as we started back to our separate rooms --

An hour later, Katie stirred in my arms. "Wow!" she breathed. "From what just happened, I think you can stop the therapy, darling. I'd love to take it over from here . . ."

So long as men in striped pants and morning coats sit around and sip tea and argue endlessly about the shape of a table; so long as other men with ribbons on their chests and gold on their caps follow the premise that legalized, mechanized, computerized destruction and death are the only answers to political disagreement, there will be Vietnams and Koreas. And Hiroshimas. Men will kill men, and be killed by other men. Women will die in bewildered innocence and never know why. Children will be born into the kind of world they don't deserve -- to grow up themselves to kill, themselves to die at the hands of other grown-up children.

There will always be people like Nora -- hurt and heart-sick, seeking to hurt in return, only to find that retaliation has the taste of ashes.

There will always be people like me, who will do what our ways of life demand that we do -- yet will find ourselves trying desperately to atone for a guilt that is not entirely our own.

And, thank God, there will always be women like Katie. Women who stand by and wait with patient serenity, for the men who go away to the wars, who lose a part of themselves in the going. Women who are willing to wait while their men seek that which the horror, the ugliness, the brutality of war has stripped away -- and help them to find it once more.

May the child Katie is soon to bear -- *my* child -- be a shining symbol of what I am trying so hard to live up to. Her love. Please, God -- may I be worthy of that love . . .

THE END

Appendix II

The Business Article

My Friends, The Salesmen

as originally published in THE OFFICE, *May 1967*

Catchy title. Tongue-in-cheek lead, setting mood for the article.

I like salesmen. Some of my best friends are salesmen. Once in a while I even take a salesman to lunch, and pay for it myself. Even though they are my friends, when I think about a few of the things certain of them have done to me through the years, I wonder how those few manage to make a living -- to say nothing of helling around in red Jaguars and taking Hawaiian vacations.

In the huge company I work for, I have a rather vague title, such as is given to somebody with little authority and much responsibility. I run a fair-to-middling sized office, replete with high and low brass, supervisors, clerical people, stenos, file clerks, and the like, all experienced and competent. My problem is to keep them happy. That means that I am responsible for everything that happens -- or doesn't happen -- up to and including the Second Coming.

Consequently, in my efforts to keep abreast of the new developments in the office equipment and administrative fields, I read everything relevant I can get my hands on, and am avidly interested in any and every new piece of equipment, every new method or new anything that turns up. Every month something does -- excellent, good, poor, bad and just plain terrible. It is my job to find out which. Therefore, there is a constant stream of salesmen, invited or uninvited, but always welcome, through my little office.

Over-view of salesmen generally.

Salesmen -- whether they be called salesmen, sales engineers, service engineers, or what have you -- have one basic mission in life, to sell their product. This is legitimate. I find no fault with it, but I wonder if the average salesman realizes that his customer may be rating him with far more severity than any sales manager could possibly evaluate him. Based on years of exposure to sales techniques, I have developed my own private rating system. Maybe it might help somebody to know what a guy in my spot has to go through, and what his reactions are.

Evaluation criteria for salesmen.

I have a friend representing a huge supply company. He is about the most pleasant chap I ever met. His line tops the field. He knows it inside and out. Tell him what you want, and he'll go to any lengths to work out a plan for you. So you give him the order. Then things begin to happen -- or not happen.

First, the material doesn't show up on schedule. His reason: the factory was down for a couple of weeks for vacation. Or the warehouse got the order fouled up. Second, when the installers arrive, the parts received do not quite fit the plan. Result: I must agree to a "few minor changes." I am stuck with an arrangement that isn't what I promised the boss. He makes a few choice remarks, both then and later, when the bill comes in. My associates come up with snide comments, and my ego takes a beating.

"Almost right" isn't good enough. I've had to accept too many "almost rights" because the job was part of a master plan, and the whole job couldn't be held up waiting to correct a miscue on my particular part of it. This kind of salesman, well-meaning and competent though he well might be, can get somebody like me into serious difficulties -- and too often does. Yet, because he does have the top of the line, he gets the business --

and in the process, gives *me* the business. But, softie that I am, I always believe that, "maybe next time . . ."

Then there is the order taker. This one also has a top grade product. He has been in my office one time, and then only in response to a telephone request for information. He was three days getting around to see me, with catalogs, samples and order book. I had talked with two other competing salesmen about the same type of equipment, but he was the only one who had the style to fit my immediate needs, so he got the order. Once more, the roof caved in on me.

First, he violated a cardinal principle of salesmanship -- never let the customer be surprised. I was surprised, but good. A week after I placed the order, I called to get a delivery date. I was told, quite casually, that "the plant was behind with orders" and it would be several weeks before my material could be shipped. No offer to try to expedite, no suggestion for interim equipment. I had a deadline to meet. Result: I spent two days fabricating makeshifts to get my job done when I had promised it. My deadline meant nothing to him. He was sorry, but . . .

Since that time, the guy has never been back. I developed, on my own, several other applications for his equipment and, being already committed to the type, I had to continue with it. Each time I had to laboriously explain to him by telephone (my call, not his) what I wanted, and to practically design the stuff myself. The only interest he seemed to have was in knowing what I was going to do with it, so he could sell others on the same idea -- selling them his equipment, naturally.

Somewhere a sales manager may be reviewing this chap's sales record, and gloating over it. My business is a part of that record -- and a pretty healthy part, too. Again, "maybe, one of these days . . ."

Another salesman friend of mine is the "guarantee boy." He, too, is in a highly competitive line, and doesn't quite have the best grade of equipment, so he tries to make up for it by promising extravagant results. His "pitch" goes something like, "Put in our equipment on test, and we will guarantee you a (bleep!) saving, or you won't owe us a penny." And this without even looking over the operation.

Of course, the reasoning behind such an approach is obvious. Once the new equipment is in place, and everybody gets used to it, all brand-new and shiny, to pronounce it no-damgood and throw it out takes a lot of moxie. The old camel-in-the-tent gimmick works pretty well, and even better if the offer is leaked to top brass who might not have the responsibility for the operation, and to whom any "guaranteed saving" looks good. Further, putting in a set of new equipment "for test" often creates a feeling of obligation on the part of the guy who gets roped into the deal -- and don't think this lad doesn't know it!

If an offer of a "guaranteed saving" is made after a realistic survey, fine. It's a legitimate sales ploy. But facts as a foundation activate my personal alarm system.

Climactic sales situation.

Probably the most irritating salesman of all is the "innuendo boy." I have run onto this type but a few times. He usually is a long-time leader in a highly competitive field, well-established and somewhat complacent.

When considering replacing existing equipment, either in kind or with other types; my policy is to call in the representative of the manufacturer of the present equipment, and tell him in complete detail what I have in mind. Most representatives welcome this, and usually have something new to tell me about something soon to be marketed by their company. Often they have changed my thinking. But not this boy!

His first response to my story is an icy stare of incredulous disbelief. Then the questions start.

"Why are you doing this to me after all these years? . . . Is anything wrong with our service? . . . Why don't you let well enough alone? . . . We have more than half the business in this country -- who are you to think that something else is better?" Then, verbatim: "I don't like the smell of this . . . just what's the real reason behind it? Kick-back, maybe? . . . Oh, well if you want that kind of equipment, we make it. But what you already have is better. . . "

The fact is that maybe he does have better equipment. That's what I call him to find out. Is this salesmanship? I think I have a better word for it.

The foregoing instances are factual. The salesmen who call on me are perhaps the best in the supply business. Personable, well educated, devoted to their companies and their calling, they honestly believe they are doing the kind of selling job they are supposed to do in the dog-eat-dog world of selling.

Concluding episode, leaving a good taste in the mouth.

I wonder what I would do, were I in their places. I couldn't sell ice water in Hades, but I believe I would use a different approach. Something like that of the old-timer who dropped in while I was in the middle of an agonizing re-appraisal of some equipment I was trying to use. Feeling plenty sorry for myself, I unburdened all over him. He smoked his pipe for a few moments, then said, "I see your problem. I've got the equipment to solve it. But I won't try to sell it to you."

I stared at him in amazement as he went on.

"Look at it this way. You've several thousand dollars worth of stuff, already paid for. I could probably talk you into throwing it all out and putting in my line -- mine would work better, too.

"But, frankly, not enough better to justify your spending the dough that the change would cost. If you'll let me, I'll show you how to make better use of what you have. Then, if you ever put up another office, maybe you'll give me a shot at it."

He did show me how to use his competitor's equipment. All he got out of it -- then -- was a steak dinner and my fervent thanks. One of these days I will have another office to set up. And who gets first crack at it? Naturally . . .

Conclusion -- sales philosophy.

Were I a sales manager, I think I would tell my salesmen, "Look, fellows. You're more than salesmen. You're sales consultants. Find out what the customer wants and needs. If you can sell him what we make, fine. If he needs something you can't furnish, don't try to snow him. Help him. Even if it means the loss of an immediate sale. He'll remember it -- and you.

"When you do get an order, volunteer a delivery date. Level with the customer. If he's got a deadline to meet, don't leave him out on a limb. Above all, don't ever let him be surprised. About anything."

Certainly such an approach would pay off with me.

THE END

Appendix III

How to Analyze the Juvenile Story

Scotty's Creek

from JACK AND JILL *magazine*

Lead character's age, name, locale of story.

Ten-year-old Scotty Lang hurried cautiously down the muddy path to the little railroad station at Big Bend, where his grandfather worked. It was awfully dark, and his flashlight made the raindrops glitter as he picked his way along the steep path. Grandfather had not come home to supper, and Grandmother had sent Scotty to find out why.

It had been raining steadily for the whole week of Scotty's visit during Easter vacation. The creeks and branches were full of water, and only that morning he had heard his grandfather say there was danger of washouts along the railroad line.

When he reached the station, his grandfather was sitting at the desk, listening to the *clickety-clack* of the telegraph sounder. "Hello, Scotty," he said. "Be real quiet until I get this message."

Scotty watched the clattering arm of the telegraph sounder, wishing he knew how to "read" what the mysterious dots and dashes were saying. Finally his grandfather opened a switch on the table, tapped the black knob of the sending key a few times, closed the switch.

Problem begins to develop.

"It's bad, Scotty," he said, and Scotty could tell that his grandfather was worried. "The track has washed out south of here. They're sending a work train down from Almas to put slag and rock in the break. All the regular trains are being side-tracked to let the work special through."

Scotty shivered with excitement. Outside it was raining

even harder. "Will there be any trouble up where the old bridge was, Gran'daddy Jack?" he asked. "You know – where they put in the big pipe and filled over it with dirt?"

"I don't think so," his grandfather said. "That's a big pipe."

A man hurried in, water streaming from his slicker. It was Mister Gass, who looked after the bridges for the railroad.

"Hello, Jack -- Hi, Scotty," he said. "I just came from Hull's Lake in my car. Hate to tell you, but the creek's pretty full right north of here, where they just put that pipe in. It seems to be holding -- but I sure wish this rain would let up."

"Listen!" Scotty's grandfather held up his hand "Do you hear anything?"

Scotty held his breath. He *did* hear something! Like rushing water -- but different from the pouring rain.

His grandfather leaned over to the window next to the track. "Oh-oh!" he said. "The water in the ditch was running *to* the creek a few minutes ago. Now it's running *away* from the creek! That means --"

Mister Gass whistled. "The creek's backed up behind the new fill. That pipe isn't big enough for a flood like this. We'd better get over there fast!"

Problem intensifies.

A jagged flash of lightning tore across the sky, a crash of thunder shook the building. The telegraph instrument, which had been chattering noisily, abruptly fell silent.

"I'd better tell the dispatcher to hold the special," Scotty's grandfather said. He opened the switch, tapped the key. Nothing happened. There was no sound from the instrument.

"That lightning burned out the line!" Grandfather's voice was tense. "Come on -- we've got to make sure the track's safe." He grabbed a red lantern and his slicker. Scotty followed the men into the downpour. They jumped the brimming ditch and hurried toward the lake that had been only a little creek. Just as they reached the bank there was a deep rumbling roar. In the lightning flashes Scotty saw the mass of earth and rock melt away under pressure of the flood. As the three watched helplessly, the earth fill disappeared, and water ran deep where the fill had been, leaving the steel rails and wooden crossties of the track hanging like a sagging ladder, swaying dizzily over the empty space where the fill had been.

Emergency develops.

Then, ever so faintly over the sullen roar of the creek and the storm, came the deep-throated whistle of a locomotive!

"The work special!" Mister Gass cried. "The engineer won't know the fill is gone! He can't see it in time to stop, with that curve in the track!"

Grown-ups can't solve the problem!

Scotty's grandfather was holding the red lantern. "I'll have to go across on what's left of the track," he said. "It's the only way." He stepped carefully onto one of the crossties that connected the rails. His weight pulled the timber free from the spikes holding it to the steel. If Mister Gass hadn't dragged him back, he would have fallen into the rushing water far below.

"It won't work, Jack," Mister Gass said. "We're both too heavy. We can only hope the engineer will see our light in time -- which isn't likely --"

But Scotty can solve it! Or try, anyway!

Scotty was scared. Swallowing hard, he tugged at his grandfather's slicker. "I'm not too heavy, gran'daddy," he said. "I can get across -- "

"No!" his grandfather said. "I couldn't let you - Scotty! Come back here!"

Scotty had grabbed the red lantern, and was already making his way out onto the swaying, quivering ladder-like thing that had been the railroad track.

"Scotty! Come back here!" his grandfather shouted again. But Scotty was inching his way across the gorge. The dim red light of the lantern was barely enough to show him where the crossties were. He held his breath as a tie shivered and creaked under his weight. It came loose, and just as Scotty managed to reach the next crosstie, the one he had been standing on splashed into the flood below him.

At last, panting, he reached the other side. He could see a glow against the dark sky -- the white glare of a locomotive headlight, the red flare of the locomotive firebox as the firemen opened the metal door to shovel coal into the roaring flames. The work special was speeding through the rainy night. There was no way for her engineer to know the deadly peril that lay before him and his heavy train.

Scotty becomes a Hero!

The deep-throated whistle sounded again. Scotty ran, stumbling and slipping on the rough slag ballast, toward the curve that seemed so far away. And just as he reached it, he was suddenly bathed in the blinding white flood of the locomotive headlight!

He stopped, stood in the middle of the track, waving his lantern frantically. In the harsh beam of the headlight, he felt terribly alone, terribly scared.

The whistle gave two piercing, screeching blasts. There was the hiss of air, the scream of metal on wet metal, as the engineer made an emergency brake application. Then, as the train came sliding toward him, wheels skidding on the slippery rains, Scotty was so frightened he couldn't move. Again the whistle screamed at him -- and just before the pilot of the locomotive reached him, Scotty flung himself from the track. He landed in a muddy ditch, his head struck something hard, and that was the last thing he remembered . . .

When he opened his eyes again, he was lying on a bunk in the caboose of the work train, big men standing all around him.

"Did -- did you see my signal in time?" he quavered.

"Sure did, sonny!" A weathered face swam into Scotty's vision. "I thought I was seeing things, having a red light waving at me on this downgrade. I slammed the brakes on, but I thought sure I was going to hit whoever was waving it. Yes, we got stopped -- with the pilot of my engine poked out over nothing but water! Sonny, you saved us from a bad wreck!"

Scotty gets a hero's reward.

A week later, Scotty stood again at the place where it had all happened. The sun was shining, and the once angry torrent was just a peaceful little creek.

Mr. Gass and some workmen were very busy, putting something on the end of the new bridge that spanned the creek. Finally he called, "All right, Scotty. Pull on this rope."

Scotty took the end of the rope Mister Gass handed him, tugged at it. A piece of canvas fell away, to expose one of the bridge nameplates the railroad used to identify streams. The nameplate read, in big, black letters --

SCOTTY'S CREEK

The workmen cheered. Mister Gass clapped Scotty on the back. But Scotty just stood there, blinking back the tears. "I d-don't know how to th-thank you, Mister Gass," he stammered. The bridge man laughed.

"Don't try. Just let us thank *you*, Scotty," he said.

Behind him, Scotty's grandfather was smiling. Scotty's heart swelled with pride. For what other grandfather had a ten-year-old grandson with a whole creek named after him?

THE END

Appendix IV

The Quasi-Humorous Personal Experience Article

My Friends, My Doctors

as originally published in KIWANIS MAGAZINE
December, 1966 - January, 1967

Editor's blurb -- and I wholly agree! States premise.
Ask any patient, Doctor; peace of mind is worth something, too!

I like doctors. I even like the crisp efficiency of hospitals. But when either or both forget that I am a humanoid-type and begin treating me like an assembly-line project, I begin to have doubts. And when I have doubts, I am unhappy.

Preamble to developing problem.

For a good many years now I have been playing nickel-and-dime with four Hippocrates' disciples. Prominent, well-heeled, middle-aged MD's, all avid poker addicts, they like to have me around because they think writers are something special, which is highly questionable, and because I try to fill inside straights, which is stupid.

Some day I'll learn to keep my big mouth shut and just play my cards. But something always slips out. Like the night I casually mentioned between deals that I was having a spot of trouble in the liquid disposal area.

Four heads turned toward me. One of the Kildares, a whiz-kid in urology who refers to himself as "The Plumber", eyed me with clinical interest, as did the bantam-legged Ben Casey who rides herd on my pet ulcer, to which I refer as "Archie."

"Look, Melvin" -- the glorified pipefitter never calls me by the same name twice - "Why haven't you done something about that? Man, you'll get out on one of those fishing trips, the pipeline will close up on you, and you'll be yelling like a pig under a fence. I'll play these."

"Yeah," chimed the gastrician. "And some day I'll have to go in after that spot of hell-fire you're nursing under your right rib-cage, and then I'll have urinary blockage to worry about, too. Nuts! Two cards."

I experienced a sinking sensation in the vicinity of the two low pair I was nursing. "Gee, thanks," I said. "You think I'd better have a once-over-lightly?"

"Elmer," said The Plumber. "You've just made yourself an appointment. Tomorrow morning, early. Bet a nick."

As I said, I talk too much. If you've ever gone through an exploratory prostatic examination, you'll know just about how much too much. By the time the next session of the four MD's and the one apprehensive free-lancer rolled around, the verdict was in. It was unanimous. Prognosis -- Trouble. BIG Trouble.

Problem specifically stated.

"Now hear this, Clyde," The Plumber was one-time Navy brass. "It's enlarged, but good. You might go for a year. Maybe less. Your deal."

I've never really recovered from having my tonsils out when I was a kid. I swallowed hard three times, looked around the table. "Fellers?" I inquired weakly. Four heads nodded.

"Well -- okay, I guess," I muttered. "But I'd sure like to know --"

"You'll know plenty, Seymour," said The Plumber. "Pikers stay out, poker's going up. Bet a dime."

Experiences detailed.

It took the combined efforts of my personal medical combine to get me into a three-bed semi-private in our local Johns Hopkins. Semi-private? So is Grand Central Station.

Being admitted for an "elective operation," which the icy-eyed lady warden at the desk implied was the next thing to a paid vacation, I was left pretty much to myself, even to putting myself to bed. I began to feel downright unwanted.

My two roomates were a B&O car inspector with a skin condition that was driving him bananas, and a retired manufacturer who had a mild coronary and was driving the nurses nuts. Good company.

The Plumber dropped in about fruit juice time. "Say, doc," I began. "About this clam-bake tomorrow. Where do you --?"

I might as well have asked for a blank check -- signed.

"Look, Andrew," he said. "If I tried to fill you in, I'd be here all night. Relax. Sack out. See you upstairs. Tomorrow."

My two cellmates surveyed me pityingly, began to regale me with Tales of Prostatectomies They'd Heard Tell Of. All with the unhappiest and the most permanent endings.

A crackling-uniformed blonde rustled in with tubes and botles, complimented me as she poked holes in my "nice, large veins." A Sonny Liston-sized orderly drifted in with a dull razor and some green soap, and what he did to me you wouldn't believe. My wife and daughter showed up with a potted plant and brave smiles. I was having a peachy time feeling sorry for myself when somebody jabbed me with a poker-sized red-hot needle, and I went to sleep in everybody's face.

Come daylight, somebody said "Roll it over, Rover," and another hot poker jabbed my you-know-what, and three minutes later I was as drunk as any wino, and as fearlessly self-assured as any James Bond facing a firing squad. I have a dizzy recollection of a white-smocked youngster trundling me up elevators and down halls as part of a long parade. Then two attendants built like wrestlers got me between them, something took a small bite out of the small of my back, and I was floating, gloriously stoned, completely divorced from reality. But my mind was never more active. Just for fun, I took the cube of three million, two hundred eighty-seven thousand, six hundred and nine, and multiplied it by the square of the hypotenuse. No mental effort at all.

The face of The Plumber swam into the pinkness around me. "Hi, Alfred," he said. "Make with the pedal extremities. Move the toes, stupid."

I got a shock. The mind said "move," but the toes said "the hell with you." From the neck down I was a side of beef.

"Doc?" I heard myself say from down in a well somewhere. "I've had it. I can't --"

"Relax, Brutus. You haven't had it, but you're going to get it. All right, gang -- let's go into this character."

Peace, 'swonderful. So is spinal anesthesia, and you may quote me. The face-masked Plumber and his henchmen and henchladies went to work on me in one of those eye-rolling huddles you see on TV. Only nobody was tense, nobody was sweating, nobody was even breathing hard -- not even me. The dialogue was good theatre, even to my critical ears.

There was a big light over the table. It was adjusted in such a way that the reflector reflected to my eyes every detail of what was going on inside me. I had a ringside seat a spectacle I would be happy to never see again. I said so, but nobody seemed to care. I joined the round-the-table conversation. I discussed politics, four-card draws, and the cellar-dwelling Washington Senators and/or Redskins. My brilliant observations on The Plumber's surgical ineptness finally got through to him; he glanced up at the overhead fixture just as I was pointing out a lousy job of hemstitching.

"Please, sir," a sweet little voice purred in my ear. "Don't interfere with the operation, okay? You're fine."

The Plumber tweaked my nose. "Okay, Jackson," he said. "We don't need you around any more. Sweet dreams, man."

Again that familiar hot-poker jab, and that was all until I woke up in bed, in the middle of what seemed to be Times Square. There were enough people around me to cheer in the New Year, but they were doing things to me that shouldn't happen to an apprentice astronaut. Bottles, tubes, tapes, hose, and who knows what else festooned all around me. I didn't mind.

I didn't anything. But I was still talking.

The Plumber's voice cut through the confusion. "Easy, Calvin. You're okay. Now, for Pete's sake, shaddup!"

So I shaddup. No pains, no gas, no nausea, no nothing until about lights-out time. My frantic efforts to reach the call bell, which had thoughtfully been placed just out of reach, alarmed my two compadres. Between the three of us -- or is it among? -- we raised such a racket that the night resident was routed out. He had been a wheel in medicine in Hungary, and now he comforted me in fluent Hungarian. "Eet ees nawthing, my fran'. Jus' a leetle ooooze. We weel watch eet. Sleep now."

"Just a *leetle!*" I howled. "Man, I'm floating in my own blood! Call my doctor! Call my lawyer!"

The night supervisor waddled starchily in, exuding disapproval. "Here, here!" she snarled, her mouth waggling. "We can't disturb people who are really sick! Hold still! There! That should hold you, cry-baby!"

I was asleep before the needle cleared my hide.

The Plumber dropped by the next morning. "Hear you had a little problem last night, Horace," he said. "Nothing unusual. Expected it. See you, Major."

Thirty seven seconds in and out. Dammit, I rated at least a two-minute briefing -- at his prices!

Next day he was back, probably a mistake. This time I was loaded for him. "Biopsy," I said. (I watch TV, too) "Report."

"Biopsy?" He frowned. "Oh. Negative. Non-malignant. 'Bye."

And I had been sweating out those two days, when one lousy word was all I needed!

Recurrence of problem.

Eight days later and considerably poorer, I went home, where I ran up a temperature that all but parboiled me. The source of my trouble closed up like a plugged sink. My wife found The Plumber at a deacon's meeting, had freckled words with him over the telephone. When she slammed the instrument down, I sighed. "I know," I said. "So I'm running a little old temperature. So keep me quiet. Give me aspirin. Let me watch the fights. Relax."

I lay around for three weeks. I received a lot of "Get-well-you-loafer" cards, developed an intimate knowledge of soap operas, got swindled by a neighbor's kid who conned me into buying a five-buck pocket radio that wouldn't even get static. I was just about to go back to work when all at once I felt like everything inside me had come loose. Once more I yelled uncle. And The Plumber said, "Happens sometimes, Junius. Relax. Use an icepack. Wear a support. See you around."

Next month's telephone bill will include one broken telephone receiver. I wrote a blind fury piece about doctors. I determined to become a dedicated crusader. I would expose Modern Medicine. And if I lived long enough to get a Medicare card, I'd burn it on the steps of the Medical Arts Center at high noon.

As a touching condescension to my delicate condition, the next session of the According to Aesculapius Chowder and Marching Society was held at my place. After the usual snide remarks about the soft life of gold-bricking writers, things got under way.

But tonight was different. I was Edward G. Robinson, Sidney Greenstreet, Humphrey Bogart and Henry Fonda rolled into one. Nickels, dimes, quarters, even some folding money began to pile up on my side of the table, accompanied by dark hints of skulduggery on my part.

Finally it came -- The Big Hand of the Evening.

The Plumber opened. I held onto an ace, queen, jack, ten, and threw away a six. After the draw I didn't look at the cards. I bet. They raised. I rasied and was raised. Still I didn't look. Finally I got four condescending calls.

"I," I said, slapping my hand over my one-card draw.

"Have words for you characters. Give ear."

Four heads turned. "You're entitled, Rhett," said The Plumber. "Feel free."

"Before I clean you guys," I said. "I want to know something. With me lying in that incredibly expensive cell, picking at the covers and staring at the ceiling, why in hell couldn't one of you -- just *one* of you -- have dropped in and said something like, "Look friend, here's the scoop. Here's what you've got, quote-end-quote. Here's what you ain't going to have any more when we get through, also quote-end-quote. And here's what also may happen -- tomorrow, next day, next month. Relax, enjoy. If you get problems, make noises. We're on your side. Why couldn't you? Why?

"And, for criminey's sake, make it the first order of business to clear up any doubt about malignancy. I'm chicken -- but I want to *know*. And so does everybody!"

There was a dead silence for a moment. The four looked at each other, then at me. Finally The Plumber said, "Okay, Enoch. We get the message. Now, we paid good money to see that screwball draw of yours. Give."

I picked up the cards. One at a time I laid them down. Ace. King. Queen. Jack. Ten. All spades. At last my inside straight had come through.

When I counted the loot that night, I found I was ahead twelve-fifty, a World War II ration token, an Atlanta bus fare slug, and two washers.

The medicos were big about it. In their medical scrawls that attest to the validity of the hand, they autographed the cards that now hang framed over my desk. And the last time they ran me through that inspection routine of theirs, they did something besides poke and grunt. They actually talked to me!

So maybe there's hope for us poor slobs who can't hold it all together, after all.

THE END

Appendix V

How to Put a Book Review Together

Locomotive 4501
as Reviewed for THE CHARLOTTE (N.C.) OBSERVER
December 29, 1968
By
Jack Clinton McLarn

Review title (sometimes included, usually written by the editor)

All Aboard For A Nostalgic Ride On The Spine-Jarring Special!

Caption: (Written by reviewer)

Locomotive 4501
by David Morgan
Kalmbach, Milwaukee
127 pages. $7.95

Reviewer's by line:

by Jack Clinton McLarn

Introductory quote from subject book:

"She's plain vanilla -- no stoker, no feedwater heater, no doodads of any sort. Just as honest an engine as you could ask. She thrives on hard work, she pleases crowds of any size and age she behaves as if half her age. It is fitting that in her old age she wears the green and gold of the Southern Railway and commands the tireless attention of so many . . ."

What the book is about:

So David P. Morgan, editor of the prestigious "rail-fan" magazine, TRAINS, sets the theme of his book. "Locomotive 4501" is many things.

It is the story of the sentimental journey of a steam locomotive, back to the scenes of her past glory -- our own Carolinas were among those scenes -- a venerable relic of an age bygone.

It is a nostalgic reminder that in the high-speed, no-nonsense world of today there are still those who look backward upon a gentler age.

And it is a picture-and-poetry record of an era that must somehow find its historian, its chronicler, its illustrator.

In some 20,650 words, often lyrical, romantic words, David Morgan, widely known as the hard-nosed editor of TRAINS, a dyed-in-the-wool champion of railroading as it used to be, tells the story, a story he lived, riding " . . . many a spine-jarring, teeth-rattling mile . . ." in the cab of Southern Railway's 4501. The story of a steam locomotive -- of her raw, brute, untamed, unpredictable personality; her many moods; her successes in the spit-and-polish world of the diesel, as well as her falls from grace, her humiliating failures.

It is the story of the men who made her odyssey possible; the men who saved her from the ignominy of the scrap docks; and the men who restored her to the world of railroading as a symbol of glory past.

If illustrated, say so:

In 170 photographs, some hauntingly beautiful works of art, some such as you and I might snap with our instamatics, many cameras have captured not only the spirit of the 4501, but the spirit of steam power itself -- the spirit of an age out of which grew the miracle of modern transportation.

If indexed, say so:

The book contains an excellent index, making it easy for the reader to find the bits of railroad folk-lore David Morgan has liberally sprinkled throughout the pages of his book.

Reviewer's evaluation of the book:

David Morgan has produced a collector's item; one to rank with the best of the railroad books on the shelves today, helping to preserve a part of Americana that deserves to be remembered and cherished.

And so long as there are small boys to stare and marvel and old men to remember and reminisce, the Age of Steam will not be forgotten. Not if the David Morgans of this world have anything to do with it.

And that is as it should be . . .

Editor's qualification of reviewer (not always done)

"*Jack McLarn is a retired railroad man who remembers with affection the sight of steam and the sound of the whistle . . .*"

Jack Clinton McLarn

Approximately
660 words

Appendix VI

Recording Script Writing

In the interest of completeness, there follows in its entirety a "cassette" recording script titled THE SALESMAN AS A "TROUBLE SHOOTER," *to illustrate a script-writing format developed and used by the author to meet the needs of some of his clients, and to exemplify the general style used in this type of sales training; a field in which the author still works.*

Tape E, Side 2

The Salesman As A "Trouble-Shooter"

		Copies for:
Voices:	3 Male	Narrator
	1 Female	Executive
Words:	2,000	Salesman
Time:	15 minutes	Secretary
		Audio Engineer

Audio:
Music up, fade to

Narrator: A frequent cause of labor trouble in industry is the "jurisdictional dispute." This is the term applied to a disagreement between workers of various crafts, when members of rival unions are unable to agree as to which craft shall perform which items of work. In some industries, notably railroads and construction, this often results in several men performing related portions of a single job when one could readily do it all. This is a wasteful, inefficient, unreasonable practice that has caused whole projects to be shut down while the wrangling went on.

Would you believe that we occasionally run onto the same wasted effort in the selling business?

Narrator: (Continuing) Before castigating me for daring to compare the exalted role of the salesman with that of the blue collar or hard-hat worker, hear me out. You're all in honored, respected endeavors, and you have more in common than you think. The salesman works hard -- with his brains, his voice, his feet. So does the railroader, the builder. Nobody has any monopoly on efficiency, performance or importance.

A buyer once mentioned to me that his company was having trouble with one of the products for which I had his account. I recall saying something like, "Sorry, I just sell the stuff. You'll have to take it up with our gripe department; that's what they're paid for."

That was asking for what I got. His reply was, "Listen, son. So far as *I'm* concerned, *you're* the 'gripe department.' You're the whole company. And if you think your responsibility ends when I sign a purchase order, you've a heck of a lot to learn about salesmanship!"

Narrator: (Continuing) Pretty ridiculous, to think that any salesman playing with a full deck would make such an asinine remark to a customer? Who would be *that* stupid? Well, I was. And, after I moved from selling into buying, you wouldn't beleive how many times I had so-called salesmen try that same cop-out tactic on me!

It's a basic for the salesman to know all there is to know about his product. It's even more of a basic that he *believe* in that product. Most salesmen work to these basics.

But far too many salesmen seem reluctant to

accept that when the salesmen takes on the selling of a commodity, he also takes on the responsibility of the commodity itself. For, so far as the customer is concerned, the salesman is the commodity, the company, the maker. He is the point of contact between the customer and the product, and for him to think that he can make his sales, draw his commission, and forget the whole thing is not only unrealistic, but downright tragic.

Narrator: (Continuing)	Now, turn the recorder off, and decide how far you think the salesman should go in the customer-company relationship.
Audio: Music bridge:	
Narrator: (Resuming)	You don't agree? The salesman should remain serenely above the battle, aloof from customer-company squabbles over quality, durability, fouled-up orders, missed delivery dates, and so on, for fear of damaging his customer "rapport" or his laboriously acquired "favored status" with the customer? You dreamer, you!
	Down inside, where it counts, you know danged well that when you sell something to a customer, you want to be proud of that sale. You want the customer to be pleased, too. And to enjoy it when things go swimmingly, only to weasel out when the storm signals go up . . . well, let's see what happens . . . We're in a buyer's office . . . (fade)

Audio:
Intercom buzz:

Executive: (Irritably) Yes, Carol?

Female Voice: (Filter) The Exeter Bearing Company man is here, sir.

Executive: (Sharply) He is, is he? Didn't think he'd have the gall to show his face around here. Send him in.

Audio:
Door opens, closes:

Salesman: (Heartily) *Good* morning, Mr. Scott! What a day! Thought you'd be out on your boat. I hear you won --

Executive: Knock it off, Clint. You got my message?

Salesman: What message? Oh -- yes, the Sales Manager did say you wanted to see me. Ready for another order so soon? That new type bearing of ours is going great --

Executive: (Interrupting) Your new type *junk*, you mean! Didn't Carson tell you how many failures we've had with those (bleep!) things?

Salesman: Well . . . he *did* say something about a little trouble you were having. But surely you're *not* blaming *me* for what that gang of misfits at the plant does. After all, I just sell the things, I don't make –

Executive: (Incredulously)	Clint, do you mean to tell me that you didn't try to find out what was wrong before you came out here? Why the (bleep!) do you think I sent for you?
Salesman:	Aw, come on, Mr. Scott. You don't have to take it out on me. I'm just a salesman. Why don't you call Charlie Womack – the Production Chief. Tell him your problem --
Executive:	Clint, I spent a lot of time and a lot of company money when you conned me into buying those blasted bearings. You made a lot of noise about "service." Now, the first time I have a complaint, you tell me to Call Charlie Womack. Mister, as far as I'm concerned, *you're* Exeter Bearnings. *You're* the guy who's gotten me in the dog-house with my boss. And if you ever expect your chicken outfit to get another bearing in this plant, you'd better shape up! I'll tell you what I think of your (bleep-bleep!) bearings . . . . (fade).
Audio: Music bridge:	
Narrator:	Wow! Does he make me feel right at home! Want to take a crack at analyzing *this* Exeter Bearings man's performance in this "complaint situation?" Turn me off while you do.
Audio: Music bridge:	

Narrator: (Continuing)

The salesman knew his customer had a legitimate complaint. Yet he used the obnoxious hail-fellow-well-met greeting; talked about unrelated matters as though attempting to minimize the seriousness of the situation. That was a major error. He should have made it immediately obvious that he was concerned about the failure of the bearings.

The salesman became personally defensive, trying to disassociate himself from any responsibility for "what that gang of misfits at the plant" had done. He even tried to avoid association with his employer, referring to himself as "just a salesman." He copped out.

Probably what was worst of all, he suggested that the customer himself take his complaint to someone else in the manufacturer's organization. If the executive needed anything more to really set him off, he had it then. And my guess is that if the bearings weren't needed desperately, the buyer would have thrown the salesman and his faulty equipment off the property.

Of course, this is an exaggerated case, to make a point. But such things do happen, and far too often.

Now, let's consider how such a situation *might* have been dealt with . . .(fade).

Audio:
Intercom buzz:

Executive: (Irritably)	Yes, Carol?
Female Voice: (Filter)	The Exeter Bearing man is here, sir.
Executive: (Sharply)	He is, is he? Didn't think he'd have the gall to show his face around here. This late, too. Send him in.
Audio: Door Opens closes:	
Salesman: (Quietly)	Good morning, Mr. Scott. I'm sorry to be so late, but I went by the plant to look at the last run on that bearing order --
Executive: (Sarcastically)	Oh, you did, did you? Right thoughty of you. Well, what're you master minds at Exeter going to do to alibi *this* snafu?
Salesman:	No alibis, Mr. Scott. How about filling me in on the trouble you're having? I didn't take too much time at the plant. I wanted to get over here and talk to you.
Executive:	We had plenty of trouble, cap! The babbit's not bonded to the brass. The lugs on the brasses are out of tram. The castings are rough . . . (fade).
Narrator:	While the buyer is chewing our salesman out, let me interrupt. The salesman -- *this* time -- is playing it cool -- letting the customer blow

	off steam. Not arguing, not justifying, just listening, and listening sympathetically. Something he *didn't* do before . . . (fade).
Executive: (Fading in)	. . . you folks just sold us a bunch of crap, mister. How do you expect us to keep up production with garbage like that, hah?
Salesman:	Babbit lining not bonded to the brass . . . Lugs out of tram . . . Castings rough . . . Mr. Scott, I don't blame you. I'd be upset .too-- and I assure you that I am. Looks as though we've let you down --
Executive:	*Let* me down? You've danged near *shut* me down!
Salesman:	I know. When I was at the plant this morning, I saw Charlie Womack. He's as shook as I am. I left him going over the whole process on your bearings. By now he should have some facts for us. May I use your phone?
Executive:	Yeah -- dial nine for outside.
Audio: Telephone dialing:	
Salesman:	Anne? Clint. Get Charlie Womack for me, will you? . . . Charlie? Clint. I'm over at Mr. Scott's office . . . You'd better believe it, he's sore . . . What did you find out about those bearings? (Pause)

	Oh? Wrong mix on the babbit? How do you suppose -- never mind . . . You're making up a new batch? Good. How about those lugs being out of tram? (Pause) Error in the customer's blue-print? Well . . . look, Charlie, they need half a dozen skids of bearings right away. Suppose you truck right over here all that you know are okay . . . Sure, I'll wait for the load. Thanks, Charlie.
Audio: Telephone replaced:	
Executive: (Sheepishly)	I'll be darned. Our print was wrong, huh? We ought to have caught that, shouldn't we?
Salesman:	No, *we* should have. And we shouldn't have goofed on the mix. By the way, Charlie tells me that the shipment before this one was a hundred percent okay. Is that right?
Executive:	Yep. Have to admit that they were good. We even put them on our stock sheets as standard.
Salesman:	Thanks for letting me know so quickly about the difficulty, Mr. Scott. We're all sorry it happened, and we'll make things right. When this is cleared up, I'd like to talk to you about using our bearings elsewhere in your operations. But right now I want to go to the delivery platform and check the new bearings in. I want to look at those rejects, too. Maybe we can correct roughness -- even might be able to machine the lugs so they can be salvaged --

Executive:	I'll go with you. We'll have lunch. And, Clint, I'm sorry I yelled at you.
Salesman: (Laughs)	Mr. Scott, in your spot I'd have yelled a lot louder and longer than you did . . .(fade)
Audio: Music bridge:	
Narrator:	Exaggerated? Of course. Just as the first scene was overdone. But I'll bet you that you won't forget either scene in a hurry.
	Turn the recorder off, and write down six things the salesman did in the second encounter to meet the complaints of the customer.
Audio: Music bridge:	
Narrator: (Resuming)	There are *six* basic steps for the salesman to take in answering *any* complaint about *any* product, whether it is registered by an irate housewife whose pop-up toaster won't pop, or an executive with a load of defective bearings, such as our explosive Mr. Scott. I'll list them for you. Compare them with your own findings.
	First, by your attitude and your words, let the customer know immediately that you take the complaint seriously. Never try to put the customer on the defensive. Be interested, be courteous, and *LISTEN*.

Second, repeat the complaint, using the customer's own words as far as possible. This does two things.

Narrator: (Continuing)

It gives you time to think. And it lets the customer hear what he said. Often what we say sounds different when we hear it repeated by someone else. And customers, particularly angry customers, sometimes have second thoughts when their words come back to them.

Third, *agree* with the customer. This may be hard to do, but find *some* area of agreement about the complaint.

Fourth, give an answer. It may be a suggestion to try another article or method, a promise to have the item re-processed or repaired. But do not imply that is was the customer's fault that the failure occurred -- even if it was.

Fifth, use the incident to create a desire on the part of the customer that can lead to a sale. Point out desirable features of other related merchandise, tell the customer of a new item to soon come out, ask permission to call the customer when it comes in. Personalize the transaction.

Sixth, close the matter out. Never leave it dangling. If the toaster is to be returned, or the shipment of bearings re-worked, have a firm understanding of what will be done. Thank the customer for his consideration, compliment him for letting you know about the complaint, and leave him feeling that you did everything you could to make things right.

Narrator:
(Continuing)

Did the first salesman do this? No. But the second? Yes, indeed. He let it be known from the beginning that he was personally concerned about the complaint. He listened while the buyer vented his anger, let him get it out of his system, without interruption. He then repeated the complaint word for word -- and agreed it was justified.

He gave an answer -- by letting the customer hear what he said to the plant on the telephone, indicating that he had nothing to hide. And when it developed that part of the foul-up was because of the customer's error, he made no effort to exploit it.

Finally, he mentioned increasing the use of the bearings, emphasizing that previous shipments had been satisfactory, to which the now mollified customer readily agreed. So the transaction was closed on a friendly note, with promise for the future.

Audio:
Music
in background:

Narrator:
(Continuing)

No salesman can be expected to always so readily overcome all errors of his company.

But he cannot sluff that duty off onto someone else. It's still within his "jurisdiction" to cope with complaints. He can, and must, "get involved." He can, and must, do everything within his power to correct errors, clear up misunderstandings, misconceptions -- anything that affects the customer-company relationship. Only when a salesman becomes irrevocably identified with the company he serves and the product he sells, and accepts the benefits and the responsibilities of both, can he be considered successful in the high calling of Salesmanship . . .

Audio:
Music up,
crescendo,
and out.

THE END

Name, address,
SS No. of
writer goes here

2,000 words
15 minutes

Appendix VII

How to Professionally Prepare a Manuscript

Manuscript format used by author in submitting work for publication, and as lecturer in writing seminars.

(Cover Page)

TITLE OF STORY OR ARTICLE

BY

YOUR NAME

Your Name	Approximately
Your Address	(How Many)
City, State, Zip	Words
SS No.	

Your Name
Your Address
City, State, Zip
SS No.

Approximately
(How Many)
Words

TITLE OF STORY OR ARTICLE
BY
YOUR NAME

This is an example of a professionally prepared manuscript, designed to attract the immediate attention of the "first readers" who screen material in editorial shops.

Allowing the indicated space at the beginning of page one of a script is for "editorial directions" to the make-up people when the material is published -- or perhaps for the editors to write you notes when they return your material. The standard format calls for about 1¼-inch margins, left, right, bottom, top, except for page one.

The word count is important. In manuscripts of up to 2,000 words, count the number of words exactly, and show the count to the nearest 100 words in the upper right corner of the first page, and at the right bottom of the cover page. For manuscripts of more than 2,000 words, count the exact number of words per page, multiply by the total number of pages, and show to the nearest 100 words.

Page No.

TITLE OF STORY
OR ARTICLE

YOUR LAST NAME

Each page of the manuscript after the first should show the title of the story article, the page number, and your last name. Manuscripts frequently become scattered in the editorial offices, and this information helps the staff in re-collating the pages.

Manuscripts should not be stapled or bound in any way. It is sufficient to "Gem Clip" them.

It is not necessary to make a "cover page" for a manuscript, as is done in this example, but it does help to keep page one clean. Dressing up submissions with fancy manuscript covers, or artistic decorations doesn't help a bit. Nor is it necessary to write an explanatory cover letter with the piece -- unless, of course, you know the editor from previous sales, in which event a short note may serve to remind that editor of previous acceptances. Most of them will remember you anyway if your work gets as far as their desks.

The "SASE" (self-addressed-*adequate*-postage *affixed*) envelope for manuscript return is a definite must in the writing business. Manuscripts of five pages or less *can* be folded and mailed in small envelopes, along with a folded return envelope, but submissions look more professional mailed flat, in a 9½ x 12½-inch envelope, with a 9 x 12-inch addressed and adequately stamped return envelope enclosed.

The book, WRITER'S MARKET, published yearly by WRITER'S DIGEST, available at local libraries, contains an invaluable section on manuscript preparation.

Page No.

TITLE OF STORY
OR ARTICLE — YOUR LAST NAME

The last page of the manuscript should not be written right down to the bottom, but should look something like the last page of this example. Editors like to have some place to write notes to their compositors -- maybe to you.

There are many "Writer's Books" published -- WRITER'S DIGEST, AUTHOR AND JOURNALIST, THE WRITER, and others. Many of them give valuable tips on new outlets for material. In the so-called "Confession" field -- probably the best outlet for the beginning writer -- WRITING THE MODERN CONFESSION STORY, by Dorothy Collett, published by THE WRITER, Boston, Mass., 02116, is good. The lady knows whereof she writes.

When you write, try to know in advance what you are going to say. Unless you are writing a scholarly essay or a "personal" article, let the characters tell the story. Let them walk, talk, breathe, laugh, weep, suffer, enjoy -- let them do something, say something. Let things keep happening. Try to make your reader believe that " . . . this could have happened to me . . .!" Maybe it could. Maybe it did.

And when you have said what you started out to say, stop. Just like this.

THE END

Your Name
Your Address
City, State, Zip
SS No. — Approximately
(How Many)
Words

Index

Chapters 5, 6
Business and Educational Writing

Chapter 7
Writing for Children -- and Kids

Chapter 8
Article Writing -- Bait, Hook, Line and Sinker

Chapter 9
"Herewith for Review"

Appendix